PLANTATION PAPERS :

PLANTATION PAPERS :

CONTAINING

A SUMMARY SKETCH

OF

The Great Ulster Plantation in the Year 1610.

BY

REV. GEORGE HILL

ISBN: 978-93-5128-771-1(HB)

First Published in 1889
Indian Reprint in 2017

Published by

Kalpaz Publications
C-30, Satyawati Nagar,
Delhi – 110052
E-mail: kalpaz@hotmail.com
Website: kalpazpublications.com
Ph.: +91-9212142040

Cataloging in Publication Data—DK
Courtesy: D.K. Agencies (P) Ltd. <docinfo@dkagencies.com>

Hill, George, 1810-1900, author.
Plantation papers : containing a summary sketch of the great Ulster plantation in the year 1610 / by Rev. George Hill.
pages cm
"First published in 1889"—Title page verso.
ISBN 9789351287711

1. Plantations—Ulster (Northern Ireland and Ireland)—History—17th century. 2. Ulster (Northern Ireland and Ireland)—History. 3. Ireland—History—1603-1625. I. Title.

DA990.U46H6 2017 DDC 941.606 23

CONTENTS.

PLANTATION PAPERS.

COUNTY OF ARMAGH.

I.

THE autumn of 1609 was a very notable one in the annals of Ulster. On the last day of July in that year the members of three Commissions came northward from Dublin, travelling together, with the Lord Deputy Chichester as their leader and guide, and accompanied by a large military force intended to prevent or repress any opposition on the part of the native populations. One Commission had been appointed to distinguish between the temporal and spiritual lands, or, in other words, to determine what lands belonged to the Crown and what to the Church throughout the six several Counties of Armagh, Tyrone, Coleraine now Londonderry, Tyrconnell now Donegal, Fermanagh, and Cavan. Another Commission was appointed to make an accurate survey or measurement of the arable lands in each county, and its work was expected to be so exactly performed that the name and situation of every balliboe, tate, quarter, and poll would be preserved and expressed on carefully prepared maps, as well as the name of every lake, river, brook, wood, bog, fort, and any other landmark throughout the said six counties. The third Commission was required to designate the precincts or baronies in each county for their several intended occupants, whether English, Scottish, servitor, or native Irish undertakers, and also to mark off the arable land in proportions of three sizes to suit planters. This last-named operation was perhaps the most difficult of all to execute, for the monastery lands, the bishops' lands, and the Church lands generally, lay intermixed with the temporal lands in almost hopeless confusion. Considering how much was to be done, and the complicated nature of the work, it is a mystery how it could be accomplished in the given time ; for, besides, and in addition to it all, assizes had to be held in each county as they passed along. The prodigious labours were commenced on the 8th of August at Armagh, and completed on the 30th of September at Cavan ! It is true there afterwards arose fierce and frequent quarrels and litigations of planters with each other, and with dignitaries of the Church, on the subject of bounds and mearings, but not greater or more frequently in this respect than might have been expected, even had the Commissioners taken a much longer period than seven weeks for their work.

The County of Armagh, in which they first commenced, comprised about 328,076 acres, English measure. It now contains eight baronies, as three have been divided since the time of the plantation, and the names of these baronies at present are Armagh, Upper Fewes, Lower Fewes, East O'Neilan, West O'Neilan, Upper Orior, Lower Orior, and Tyrany. The Commissioners found that several lands in this county could not be claimed for the Crown, and consequently could not be made available for plantation purposes. As such lands lay chiefly in the two baronies of Armagh and Tyrany, the Commissioners of Survey, and the Commissioners appointed to mark off the proportions, had only to devote themselves to the three other baronies of Oneilan, Orior, and the Fewes. The Commissioners whose duty it was to determine what lands in each county were vested in the Crown reported in reference to Armagh that "All the lands of the said county are now in the real and actual possession of the

Crown, except the demesne lands belonging to the Archbishop of Armagh; and except the inheritance of the heirs of Sir Nicholas Bagnall, deceased, in the barony of Orier and in the barony of Oneilan; and except the inheritance of Sir Tirlagh MacHenry O'Neill, lying in the barony of the Fewes; and except the inheritance of the heirs of Sir Henry Oge O'Neill, deceased, in the barony of Tyrany; and except the lands belonging to the Dean of the cathedral church of Armagh, or to the prior and vicars choral of the same church, or to the Abbey of St. Peter and St. Paul; and except the inheritance of Marmaduke Whitechurch and Patrick M'Felomy O'Hanlon."

With respect to the several exceptions mentioned in the foregoing passage from the Commissioners' report a few explanatory remarks may be necessary. In the "Abstract of Titles," drawn up by Sir John Davys, the Attorney-General, who was very actively engaged on this Commission, he says—"And now by virtue of a commission taken at Armagh, 12th August, 1609, to inquire of the ecclesiastical lands in that and other counties, and to distinguish the same from the lands of the Crown, it is found that the Archbishop of Armagh is seised, in right of his archbishoprick, of 26 townes, or thereabout, as of his mensal or demesne lands, and that he ought to have certain perpetual rents and other duties out of 160 townes more (which are not found to be termon or herenach lands), lying in several territories of this county; but the tenants thereof being now Irish are found to be inheritors thereof time out of mind, according to the Irish customs of tanistry and gavelkind; and that the Lord Primate could not remove the said tenants at his pleasure." Sir Tirlagh MacHenry O'Neill, of the Fewes, was brother-in-law of Hugh O'Neill, the great Earl of Tyrone; and Sir Henry Oge O'Neill was the Earl's son in-law. Although both had held their lands from the Earl as chief or head of the whole Clann

O'Neill, yet they deserted him, and got grants of their lands from the Crown in their own name. Sir Henry Oge's loyalty to the Government induced him to volunteer against O'Dogherty in 1608, and during that brief conflict of only three months' duration he (Sir Henry) and his eldest son were slain. His lands lay on both sides of the Blackwater, part of his large estate being in the barony of Tyrany, County Armagh, and the other and larger part on the western bank in Tyrone. This latter portion was known as Munnterbirn, now Caledon; and Sir Henry Oge's grandson was the Felomy Roe O'Neill of 1641. Sir Tirlagh had also a large estate in the Fewes. He had owned also the well-known Galloglass lands, in the small barony of Armagh, which had been appropriated by the Government, and he wanted compensatory lands in the barony of Tyrany for this loss. Chichester was willing to make some allowance in the shape of more bounds—larger territory—if Sir Tirlagh would remove to the County of Cavan, but he preferred remaining in the Fewes, although about to be hemmed around there by Scottish settlers, rather than risk any surrender of his ancestral estate.

As to the exception of lands belonging to the dean, Davys explains in his "Abstract of Titles" thus:—"There are but three towns and odd sessiagh's found to belong to the Dean, but there are nine towns and odd sessiaghs found to belong to the vicars choral, to which we think he has no title; howbeit the jurors cannot find that the said lands at any time were in the possession of the said dean and prior, but that the said book (an old book shown to the jurors by the dean) mentions that there was paid out of the town of Dromagh six shillings, one mutton, and one lossett of butter unto the prior; and rents to the dean out of the other lands." According to Chichester's opinion the Church machinery there was not in a hopeful condition when he had visited

Armagh in the autumn of 1605. "And first, in the church there," he writes to the Council in London, "which was much ruined and fallen to decay, we found a number of priests, all ordained by foreign authority, and holding their dignities and prebends by bulls from Rome—not one man amongst them disposed to celebrate Divine service and sacraments according to his Majesty's laws. We found also that certain tithes of great value, intended for the support of a college of twenty-two vicars choral of that church, were demised in lease by Mr. Wood without any lawful authority." At least twenty townlands of the Abbey of St. Peter and St. Paul were granted to Sir Toby Caulfield; the Bagnall family held Church lands in the two baronies of Oneilan and Orier; Whitechurch had a grant of six townlands belonging to the Abbey of St. Peter and St. Paul; and O'Hanlon had a good service grant of twelve townlands, on condition that three were to be surrendered, if required, to Captain Atherton for the fort of Mountnorris.

Whilst some Commissioners were thus attending to the grave question of titles to property, others were engaged in measurements, and others in marking off the proportions. They commenced with the barony of Oneilan, which was more frequently and anxiously sought after by undertakers than any other, from the well-known fertility of its soil, and also because of its nearer proximity to the Pale than any of the other baronies. This barony, which is now divided into East and West Oneilan, then contained two sections also, which were known respectively as Clancann and Clanbrazill. East Oneilan contains 34,498 statute acres, and West Oneilan 59,502. The former includes part of the parishes of Magheralin and Shankill, with the whole of the parishes of Seagoe and Muntiaghs; its towns are Lurgan and part of Portadown, and its principal village is Charlestown. West Oneilan contains the whole parishes of Drumcree and Tartaraghan, with part of the parishes of Newry, Armagh, Clonfeacle, Grange, Killyman, Kilmore, Loughgall, and Mullaghbrack; its towns and villages are Richhill, Loughgall, Derryscollop, Maghery, Milltown, and part of Portadown.

In this fine sweep of territory the surveyors only found 16,500 acres, plantation measure, of arable land; whilst all the vast remainder was set aside as unprofitable, or, at least, described by them as such. The arable land in Oneilan was marked off into 13 proportions—eight of 1,000 acres each, three of 1,500 acres each, and two of 2,000 acres each; and this whole quantity was distributed, with some slight exceptions, among ten English undertakers or planters. The vast scopes of what were called waste or unprofitable land adjoining or surrounding the several proportions were thrown in gratuitously with these proportions, and this arrangement was observed throughout all the other counties; so that an undertaker who got a proportion of 1,000 acres, or 1,500 acres, or 2,000 acres, became in this way the owner of three, five, or even ten times as much land as was conveyed in his grant. But these vast additions were by no means unprofitable; they consisted of bogs, woods moorland, or fields that had been under cultivation before the war, but were permitted during that disastrous conflict to become partially hidden by whins and briars. These incumbrances were easily removed, and the tenant settlers often found such patches even more remunerative than their arable acres; for the fields thus cleared, having had time to rest, yielded their golden harvests promptly, and in many cases abundantly. The moorland portions always supplied ample and wholesome pasturage for young cattle; the woods soon became sources of comparative wealth to their owners, as timber was required in all directions for building purposes; and even the bogs were found indispensable as affording unfailing supplies of fuel in the shape of bogwood and peat.

The names of the English undertakers, or planters, in Oneilan were Richard Rolleston, clerk; Francis Sacherville, Esq.; John Brownlowe, Esq.; James Matchett, clerk; William Powell, Esq; John Dillon, Esq.; William Brownlowe, Esq.; William Stanhowe, gentleman; John Heron, gentleman; and Sir Anthony Cope, knight. After the first twelve months' occupancy Sir George Carew was sent specially by order of the King to inspect the plantations in Ulster, and to report either progress or non-progress in every individual undertaker's proportion.

II.

The following is Carew's report from O'Neilan: —" The Lord Saye and Seale, 3,000 acres; has made over his portion to Sir Anthony Cope, knight, who has sent over a very sufficient overseer named William Pearson, with another to assist, who are resident. They have begun a fair castle of freestone, and other hard stone, fourteen or fifteen workmen and nine carpenters employed; great part of the freestone for the coynes and windows is prepared four or five miles beyond Armagh; two English carts or teams with horses and oxen attend the drawing of the materials; there are twenty muskets and callivers, with competent furniture ready on all occasions; the way for carriage of timber, which is five miles, is made passable, and so is the way to the freestone, which is eight miles from the place; two of the principal workmen to be made freeholders, the rest are to have land upon reasonable terms; sixteen mares and horses employed in the carriage of materials. John Brownlow, 1,500 acres, and his son, William Brownlow, 1,000 acres; both resident and dwelling in an Irish house; have brought over six carpenters, one mason, a tailor, and six workmen; one freeholder and six tenants on their land; preparations to build two bawns; some muskets and other arms in readiness. Mr. Powell, 2,000 acres; has put over his land to Mr. Roulstone; no freeholders nor artificers are drawn upon it, nor work done, save the building of two bays of a house. When we were in the North, one William Banister presented himself before us as an agent for Powell, and said that preparations were being made for building a house and bawn, and that divers Englishmen had promised to come over and inhabit his land. Francis Sachervill, 2,000 acres; is resident; has brought over three masons, one carpenter, one smith, nine labourers, and two women; four horses and a cart; no freeholders nor other tenants; has drawn stone and other materials to the place where he intends to build. Sachervill adds that he has built three houses and placed tenants in them, and is building a stone house, and has competent arms in his house. Mr. Stanhawe, 1,500; was here, took possession, and returned into England; his son, Stephen Stanhawe, is overseer in his absence; has done nothing. Mr. James Matchett, 1,000 acres; his eldest son, Daniel Matchett, age twenty-four years, agent; resident since Michaelmas, 1610; two freeholders upon the land, but no tenants or labourers; has begun a bawn, and intends to finish it before Allhallowtide, and to effect what is required by the articles; has provided materials for buildings; has nine horses and other beasts ready to draw the same to his work; has arms for ten men. Mr. John Dillon, 1,500 acres; is resident, with his wife, children, and family; brought over twelve Englishmen, with their wives, children, and servants; fifty-two English cows, fifteen horses for work, six carpenters, three masons, seven labourers, and two women servants; has felled oaks, small and great; has built a strong bawn, with houses for lodgings and to keep provisions in; and is well stored with arms and munition. Mr. Roulstone, 1,000 acres; is resident; has timber buildings after the English fashion; three men of good sort resident, who shall be freeholders, whereof one has built a house of stone and clay; seven poor Englishmen, with their wives and children, and some servants who are to be tenants; they have four English cows and eight horses for ploughing among them all."

The foregoing is perhaps the most favourable report of progress in planting which Carew was able to make during his peregrinations in Ulster in the autumn of 1611. 1. Richard Rolleston, who got a proportion of 1,000 acres called Teemore, was a parson, and came from Staffordshire. He represented himself as having an income of £100 a year, and "goods" which might be valued at £500. So far as his place of settlement was concerned, his lines may be said to have fallen pleasantly enough, for his manor of Teemore was near Loughgall. Perhaps, however, his profession may have disqualified him for the special work of a planter, as he very soon got into financial difficulties, and placed himself in the hands of an Englishman from Stoke-Pogis, named Francis Annesley, who relieved him of his manor in a rather unceremonious style. Annesley came originally as a servant in the household of Chichester, and, having saved his earnings, was able to lend cash advantageously. He got a mortgage for £420 against the poor parson's "proportion," and, by foreclosing summarily, shut off the latter from any further share or care as an owner of land. 2. Francis Sachervill came from Rossbye, in Leicestershire, representing himself as worth £300 a year. He got two proportions of 1,000 acres each, called Mullalelish and Leggacurry, and resided in the latter until the time of his death, which happened in 1649. Before that date he had sold all his lands, the proportion called Mullalelish passing soon afterwards into the hands of Sir William Alexander, of Menstrie, a Scottish speculator in plantations. Sir John Scot, of Scotstarvet, a rather caustic critic on some of his contemporaries, makes the following entry in reference to the Knight of Menstrie:—"He got great things from his Majesty, as especially a liberty to create a hundred Scotsmen knights, baronets, from every one of whom he got £200 sterling; he also got a liberty to coin base money, far under the value of the weight of copper, which brought great prejudice to the kingdom—at which time he built his great lodgings [castle] at Stirling, and put on the gate thereof *Per mare, per terras*, which a merry man changed to *Per metres, per turners*, meaning that he had attained to his great estate by poesy and that gift of base money. The King also honoured him with the title of the Earldom of Stirling." 3. John Brownlowe came from Nottingham, and obtained 1,500 acres named Dowcoran, which was created a manor of the same name. So long as he lived he faithfully carried out the conditions on which he received his lands. He built his castle and bawn on a townland of his property named Derry or the Oak Wood, and called it Brownlowe-Derry. At his death his son William succeeded. 4. James Matchett was a parson, and came from Tremingham, in the County of Norfolk. He got the proportion of Kernahan, which he was unable to retain, and which he sold to Sir Oliver St. John, who had got lands at Tanderagee. Matchett was slain during the first breaking out of the insurrection of 1641. 5. William Powell is described in his grant as "of Castleparke, within the honour of Tutbery, in the County of Stafford." This undertaker, who got a proportion of 2,000 acres, was one of several brothers who had all situations in various departments of the King's service. His proportion of Balliworran lay on both sides of the Upper Bann, and occupied the southern extremes of both the subdivisions known as Clanbrassill and Clancann, in

O'Neilan. He soon sold his lands to Michael O'Bynns or Obbyns, of Balliworran, *alias* Portadown. 6. John Dillon was also a native of the County of Stafford, and got a middle-sized proportion of 1,500 acres, called Mullabane, which was created a manor of the same name. He appears to have been among the most energetic and successful undertakers in the district. His residence, which he named Castledillon, stood about a mile and a half northward from Armagh, and in the centre of his own manor. 7. William Brownlowe, the son of John Brownlowe already noticed, owned a small proportion of 1,000 acres named Ballynamoney, created into a manor of the same name. On the death of his father, William Brownlowe became the owner of the two proportions of Dowcorran and Ballynamoney, which lay side by side, and were at first undertaken by both respectively. William, the son, died in 1660, leaving his carefully managed property to his daughter, Letitia Brownlowe, *alias* Clinton, during her life, and afterwards to his nephew, Arthur Chamberlain. 8. William Stanhowe came from Norwich, and got a middle proportion called Kannagolah created a manor, also so named. He had asked for lands "in O'Neilan only," as several other undertakers had done, and lived in his new home until the time of his death in 1635. He was succeeded by his son Henry, who was known as of Clontilawe, County of Armagh. The proportion of Kannagolah lay in the old Irish territory of Clancann, stretching nearly its whole length from north to south. A portion of Kannagolah adjoined the south-western shore of Lough Neagh, the Upper Bann separating it on the east, from Ballywarren or Portadown. 9. John Heron's native place in England is not recorded. He got two proportions of 1,000 acres each, named respectively Aghivillan and Broughes, created into a manor retaining the same names. He died in 1616, and was succeeded by his brother, Sir Edward Heron.

10. **Sir Anthony Cope** purchased his two proportions of Dirrichreeny and Dromully, from Lord Saye and Seale or Sele, the first patentee. Cope was born in Cope Castle, afterwards Holland House, and belonged to a well-known English stock. His lands included Loughgall, *alias* Tullyard. He died in 1630, and his son Henry, who succeeded him, died when a boy, and was succeeded by a younger brother, Anthony, who died in 1642.

Among the natives of high rank who were removed from O'Neilan to make way for these Englishmen was Arthur or Art, a son of the first Baron O'Neill, of Dungannon. To distinguish him from other O'Neills bearing the same Christian name, he was known generally as Art MacBaron. He was known also as a man who had devoted himself to the peaceful pursuits of life, in the midst of almost incessant tumult and war. Oneilan does not, as might be supposed, derive its name from the O'Neills, but from a chieftain of the Clann Colla, named Niallan, who lived before the O'Neills had become supreme in Ulster. When they became the ruling power, however, Oneilan was found to be one of the most attractive districts in their Principality; and some or indeed several members of the leading family in their generations made it their favourite place of abode. Oneilan was always regarded as set apart to be the home of the eldest son or brother of The O'Neill, as the case might be; the supreme chieftain, or head of the family, however, who generally dwelt at Dungannon, reserving to himself the right of sojourning during a part of the year by the shores of the charming Loughgall. This lough was formerly much more extensive that, at present, and contained an artificial island, on which was built a lake-dwelling, used generally as a summer residence, and always as a sort of refuge in times of peril. As Art or Arthur O'Neill was the eldest son of the Baron, he had always occupied Oneilan as a matter of course, although his younger half-brother, the great Earl of Tyrone, from the time he became the representative of the family, often claimed his right of temporary residence there. In fact, Hugh O'Neill frequently resided in Oneilan in preference to Dungannon, enjoying, perhaps, more congenial society in the former, and greater opportunities for rest at intervals from the turmoil which sadly characterised Ulster life in his day. In an old map of this province, about the year 1560, Oneilan is mentioned as "Art Mac Baron his Countree," and the lake dwelling is described as "Lough Galle, Art Mac Baron his chiefe house and houlde." This position was always gazed at with longing eyes by the English of the Pale, who rejoiced when any pretext offered them an opportunity of breaking from their enclosures for a raid over its green fields and among its comfortable homesteads.

In this Ulster paradise Art Mac Baron brought up a numerous family of sons and daughters. Two of his elder children were the gallant but ill fated Brian MacArt, and Ellis or Alice, the heroic wife of Con O'Neill, of Castlereagh, near Belfast; and two of his younger children were the celebrated Owen Roe Mac Art, and a sister who married Philip O'Reilly, the chief or head of his tribe, who dwelt in Loughouter Castle, County of Cavan. Brian Mac Art was styled by native chroniclers the "Bright Star of his Tribe," and was feared and watched more closely by Government agents and officials during the war with the Northern Earls than any other leader in Ulster—not even excepting the Earl of Tyrone himself. When the Northern chiefs of septs in several districts began to grow weary of the dreadful struggle, and to show symptoms of surrender, Brian Mac Art with his flying column stirred them up in all directions—in the Ards, in Lecale, at Dromore, in Kilwarlin—and soon convinced them that it would be safer for them to stand firm than to flinch. The Government came to the conclusion that at the old Earl's death, or perhaps sooner, Brian Mac Art would become The O'Neill, as a matter of course; but soon after the struggle ended. He was done treacherously to death, and so vanished all fears of his succession. His name still survives—*stat nominis umbra*—in Mac Art's Fort, and in the locality now known as Ballymacarrett.

III.

The organisers of plantation in Ulster wisely concluded that it would be prudent, politically speaking, to give small grants of land to several persons among the native nobility and gentry who had remained quiescent during all the planting arrangements, and especially to such as had made no hostile movements at the time of Sir Cahir O'Dogherty's insurrection in 1608. It added, no doubt, greatly to the work of the Commissioners to mark off so many small shreds of land in those precincts or baronies allotted to such native gentry as had obtained them; but even a greater difficulty was expected in having these grantees removed from their own cherished homes into barren districts, where they would have none of the comforts of life, and no means of providing them. The Council in London, without knowing or caring much about the matter, depended on Chichester's powers of solving all such little questions affecting the natives. They issued their mandate, therefore, confidently, although, in some respects, cautiou-ly, as follows :—"The Lord Deputy to take order for the removing of the natives presently, with as little trouble as may be, for making an easy way for the plantation. And, if he see cause, he may transplant them from one county to another, which, being a matter of the greatest moment, will require the greatest and most serious consideration."

The original condition was that these natives getting small patches should be removed to barren districts, but within their native counties. In the foregoing "instruction," however, which was doubtless suggested or asked for by Chichester himself, he is permitted to transplant them into other counties, should such be found necessary in the interests of the plantation.

Chichester had some difficulty in bringing himself to face this question of removing the native gentry, notwithstanding his natural obtuseness, and, although he had an army in readiness "to withstand and suppress them if they will not otherwise be brought to reason." He was greatly disquieted also at this crisis by a communication received from Sir Toby Caulfield, who had been commissioned to hunt after and destroy as many woodkerne as possible in the Fewes Woods, and who had utterly failed in his mission because of the general sympathy of the people with the hapless woodkerne, driven from their estates, and obliged by stern necessity to follow in the footsteps of Robin Hood. Caulfield writes to Chichester as follows:—"There is no hope of the people since the news of the plantation, that it will shortly be many of their cases to be woodkerne out of necessity, no other means being left them to keep a being in this world than to live as long as they can by scrambling. They also hope that, the summer being spent before the Commissioners come down, so great cruelty will not be offered as to remove them from their houses upon the edge of the winter, and in the very season when they are to supply themselves in making their harvest. They hold discourse among themselves, that if this course had been taken with them in war time it had had some colour of justice; but they having been pardoned and their lands given them [in 1603], and having lived under law ever since, and being ready to submit themselves to mercy for whatever offence they can be charged with since their pardoning, they conclude it to be the greatest cruelty that was ever inflicted on any people. I take leave to assure you there is not a more discontented people in Christendom." When Chichester, however, had screwed his courage at last up to the necessary pitch, on receiving instructions from England, he snatched his pen and wrote to Salisbury, as if anxious to claim a religious sanction for his conduct, thus—"Now, upon receipt of his Majesty's directions, and those from yourself and the Council, I intend, by God's permission, to be at the Cavan on St. James's Day, the 25th instant, there to begin that great work on the day of that blessed Saint in heaven and great Monarch on earth [James I], to which I pray God to give good and prosperous success, for we shall find many stubborn and stiff-necked people to oppose themselves against and to hinder the free passage thereof, the word of removing and transplanting being to the natives as welcome as the sentence of death. Most of the Commissioners named in the King's letter have prayed to be excused from personal attendance in the journey, as well by reason of age and impotence of body as of the difficulty of the ways, the foulness of the weather, and the ill lodging they shall find in Ulster." This letter, which commences so heroically, closes by informing Salisbury that the writer has "in readiness some dogs and mewed hawks which shall come to you as soon as they are fit to be carried so far; the soar hawks are for the most part so rotten that I think it the better course to send you such as are tried and mewed henceforth, though they be fewer. They are poor presents for so rich a benefactor."

When such was naturally the profound feeling of excitement and fear, even amongst those who had got small but wholly inadequate patches to offer even some faint hopes of being able barely to live, it was thought good policy on the part of the removers to handle Art Mac

Baron somewhat gently, so that he might be persuaded to remove quietly, and thus become a peace-loving model for the imitation of all his humbler kinsmen and neighbours and tenants in Oneilan. Chichester was brought to admit that such natives of rank as had escaped the gallows or transportation to Sweden or to Virginia in America, required some small means of support, but he pretended to decline taking any part in locating such natives, or being made in any degree responsible for their future loyalty to the Throne. In this case, however, he was ostensibly relieved, for the Council in London took upon themselves the task of deciding that the aged chieftain was to be removed to the adjoining barony of Orier, and there to have a life interest in 2,000 acres. Art Mac Baron was too old and feeble to offer even a word of remonstrance, and the only request he made was that the lands might be granted to his wife and himself, so that should he die before her she might not be left utterly destitute. With this very modest request Chichester magnanimously recommended the Council to comply, for O'Neill's wife was as old as himself, and both were literally tottering on the brink of the grave. The deputy, however, sustained the simple petition before the Council only on the grounds that granting it would induce O'Neill to remove from Loughgall more resignedly, his example thus operating, as Chichester expressed it, "as a great furtherance towards the removal of the rest of the natives." This small concession appears to have had the much desired effect, for in the month of December, 1609, he informs Salisbury by letter that "Art Mac Baron's example in accepting his portion, and his removing from his long-continued habitation by promise, at May next, has prevailed with the multitude according to my expectation, so that I think we will sooner remove most of the natives than bring others with goods and stocks to sit down in their places."

In this expression of opinion as to the probable dearth of applicants for the confiscated lands in Ulster, Chichester was entirely mistaken. Great numbers, anxious to become undertakers, or, in other words, to have shares in the land spoil, had to be sent empty-handed away. No fewer than four "consorts" or companies, headed respectively by Sir Francis Anderson, Sir William Moneon, Sir Maurice Barcley, and Lord Saye and Sele, came promptly forward as applicants for lands "in Oneilan only." There was no lack of urgent suppliants (such as they were) for homes in Ulster, both of the landlord and tenant classes. An old and honest chronicler, the Rev. Andrew Stewart, Presbyterian minister of Donaghadee, tells us in his well-known manuscript, of the seething multitudes that came across the Irish Sea and the North Channel to our shores. "From Scotland," says he, "came many, and from England not a few; yet all of them, generally the scum of both nations, who for debt, and breaking and fleeing from justice, or seeking shelter [from charges of manslaughter in their clan-fights], came hither, hoping to be without fear of man's justice in a land where there was nothing, or but little as yet, of the fear of God. And in a few years there flocked such a multitude of people from Scotland that these northern counties of Down, Antrim, Londonderry, &c. [including five other counties of Ulster], were in a good measure planted." Some years after the first rush of settlers, in 1609-10, there came another flight, of whose movements we have a brief but interesting notice by the well-known tourist or traveller Sir William Brereton, who visited and described several places throughout the British Isles. In the course of his peregrinations, Brereton found himself at the town of Irvine, in Ayrshire, where he was the guest, for a time, of a Scottish minister named Blair. The latter informed Brereton of a great exodus that had taken place from Scotland. "Above ten thousand persons," said he, "have, within two years last past, left this country wherein they lived, which was betwixt Aberdeen and Inverness, and are gone for Ireland; they have come by one hundred in a company through this town, and three hundred have gone hence together, shipped for Ireland at one tide. None of them can give a reason why they leave this country; only some of them who make a better use of God's hand upon them have acknowledged to mine host in these words that it was a just judgment of God to spew them out of the land for their unthankfulness. One of them I met withal and discoursed with at large, who could give no good reason, but pretended the landlords increasing their rents; but their swarming in Ireland is so much taken notice of and disliked as that the Lord Deputy has sent out a warrant to stay the landing of these Scotch that come without a certification."

In this passage Brereton refers, as already stated, to a somewhat later movement than that of 1610, and his statement is interesting as giving us glimpses of a very poor but much more worthy class of colonists than those who came in that year, with a rush, as if the mother country had flung them forth in anger. And such was indeed the fact, for the original lot, with rare exceptions, had evidently parted with their "auld respected mither" very much for her respectability and peace. Such, also, was the testimony respecting them of Josias Welsh, the grandson of John Knox, who was placed for a time as Presbyterian minister at Templepatrick, and who mentions that in a period of about seven months, during his ministry, "God had taken by the heart hundreds that never knew Him before." When people of the class thus described by Stewart and Welsh found that they had really escaped from their troubles in Scotland, and alighted in Ulster on much better lands than they had ever known before—when they felt, moreover, that they were thoroughly protected in their new homes, and even patted by Government officials all around—it would reasonably occur to them that Providence had a hand in their deliverance, and that, as they now really "felt the way of the transgressor hard," it would be better to cease from leading the lives of lawless outcasts, and become thrifty and law-abiding colonists. And they did so; as our faithful chronicler Stewart tells us in his own quaint style, thus:—"Yet most of the people, as I said before, made up of a body, and it is strange, of different names, nations, dialects, temper, breeding; and, in a word, all void of godliness, who seemed rather to flee from God in this enterprise than to follow their own mercy; yet God followed them when they fled from Him—albeit at first it must be remembered that they cared little for any Church." But it must be remembered also that their lands, which had rested during the war, soon yielded these newcomers such golden harvests that on reaping the first season's crops they had enough and to spare; so that when their poor kinsmen who dwelt between Aberdeen and Inverness found that they could send food from Ulster on cheaper terms than it could be raised in Scotland, they forthwith sold out and came hither also.

IV.

Although Chichester had not the time or perhaps the disposition to criticise the rank and file in the movement too closely, he anxiously scanned the undertakers, as he occasionally found opportunities of doing. He had already so much toil, and worry, and even terror at times, in carrying forward the work so far, that he felt naturally very deeply interested in the parties on whom it would be mainly dependent in the future. His first impressions of the planters were not favourable, as he explained, when writing to Salisbury in November, 1610. "Those from England," said he, "are for the most part plain country gentlemen, who may promise much, but give small assurance or hope of performing what appertains to a work of such moment. If they have money they keep it close, for hitherto they have disbursed but little; and, if I may judge by outward appearance, the least trouble or alteration of the times here will scare most of them away. It is said by themselves that, of the parties at first to be undertakers, some have exchanged their proportions, and others sold them outright. In one precinct [O'Neilan] of those that have appeared two are churchmen [parsons], and one a youth of some eighteen or nineteen years." "The Scottishmen," he continues, "come with greater port, and better accompanied and attended, but it may be with less money in their purses; for some of the principal of them, upon their first entrance into their precincts, were forthwith in hand with the natives to supply their [the Scottish planters] wants; and in recompense thereof promise to get license from his Majesty that they [the natives] may remain upon their lands as tenants unto them, which is so pleasing to that people [the Irish of Ulster] that they will strain themselves to the uttermost to gratify them, for they are content to become tenants to any man rather than be removed from the place of their birth and education."

The Deputy was thus specially jealous of anything approaching to fraternisation between the new-comers and the natives, for in this he saw the eventual repudiation of his own policy of permitting no Irish to remain on the proportions or scopes of arable lands granted to the undertakers. And that policy had eventually to be altogether repudiated in the interests of the undertakers or landlords themselves, the repudiation commencing so early as 1630, when estates were regranted with the proviso that their owners could each let a third part of his lands to native tenants, and take on native labour *ad libitum*. Even in his own time, and with his own eyes, Chichester saw the evil result of his policy in the general wreck caused throughout Ulster at the very first attempt to carry out his plantation programme. The whole property of the Irish—from the chief down to his humblest tenant—consisted in cattle, so that, when the lands throughout Ulster were lost to its inhabitants, their cattle became of little or no value, and had to be handed over—nominally sold—to the new tenants now crowding into their houses and fields. Some of the native gentry who had been granted small patches of freehold struggled for a time to retain possession of very much reduced herds; but the natives generally, including nearly all who had become grantees, were obliged before removing to sacrifice their property to a deplorable extent. Even this great misfortune, however, becomes a special ground of suspicion and complaint against them by Chichester in his anxiety to make his victims responsible for the results of his own evil policy. In a letter to his patron, Salisbury, he writes as follows:—"They sell away both corn and cattle, and when they are demanded why they do so, their answer is that they know not what to do with them, nor to what place to carry them, the portion of land assigned to each of them [*.i.e.*, to the few who had got little portions] being too small to receive and feed them. They seek by all means to arm themselves, and have undoubtedly some pieces in stone, and more pikes, and thereof can make more daily; but powder and lead are scarce with them. I will do my best to prevent their revolt, but greatly doubt it, for they are infinitely discontented." Of all the planters who came to Ulster only three or four brought with them a very trifling amount of stock, both they and their tenant-settlers well knowing that the natives had lots of cattle, and that they could more easily supply themselves in Ulster than anywhere else. Several of the natives getting tiny grants refused to accept them, stating as a valid reason for their refusal that they would prefer "being tenants at will to the servitors, who had sufficient scopes to receive them, than freeholders from the Crown of such small parcels, for which they should be compelled to serve in juries, and spend double the yearly value thereof at assizes and sessions."

We now return to the Commissioners, from whom we parted company as they passed from Oneilan to the Barony of the Fewes. They were shut out of the two baronies of Armagh of Tyrany, which contained very extensive church lands and lands belonging to the heirs of Sir Henry Oge O'Neill. In passing into the barony of the Fewes they found that vast sweeps of it were wooded, and that a large section of its lands belonged to Sir Tirlagh MacHenry O'Neill. This immense barony was anciently known as Fiodha, or the "Wooded," a word which we now endeavour to represent by our term Fewes. The old Irish territory so called is comprised in the two modern baronies, and we may form a general idea of its extent by looking at it as a long upland stripe reaching from the neighbourhood of Richhill to the south-western extremity of the County of Down. In the upper division of the Fewes are the parishes of Ballymyre and Newtonhamilton, with part of the parishes of Creggan and Lisnadill. Its only towns are Newtonhamilton and Crossmaglen. The lower division of the Fewes contains part of the parishes of Kilclooney, Lisnadill, Loughgilly, and Mullabrack. Its only town is Markethill, and its principal villages are Belleek and Hamilton's Bawn. The two divisions taken together contain upwards of 77,000 English acres. In the portion belonging to the Crown the Commissioners could only find 6,000 arable acres, which were marked off into five proportions, and afterwards distributed by lot amongst five Scottish undertakers.

The names of these five gentlemen were Sir James Dowglasse, knt.; Henry Acheson, gent.; Sir James Craig, knt.; William Lawder, gent.; and Claude Hamilton, gent. After they had been twelve months in possession of their respective proportions, Sir George Carew reported of them as follows:—"Sir James Dowglasse, knight, 2,000 acres; George Lawder is his deputy; has done nothing. Claude Hamilton, 1,000 acres; is building a stone bawne with round flankers, twenty-four yards square, and a wall eight foot high; has raised stone to finish the bawne, and to make a stone house, and has drawn trees to the building; is now building three houses, one forty-eight feet long; five families, sixteen men and women of British [Scottish] birth, are upon the land, whereof six are masons; eighty cows and fourteen horses and mares in stock. William Lawder, 1,000 acres; Alexander Lawder, resident agent; certain houses built and repaired wherein ten families and three servants, to the number of eighteen are residing; eighteen horses and mares and sixty cows; stone raised and timber felled. James Craige, 1,000 acres, resident, has begun to build a mill; sown and reaped oats and barley; built some tenements wherein are placed some families of British. Henry Acheson, 1,000 acres, has raised stone and felled timber; has eight or nine people, who have thirty cows and fifteen horses and mares, with some arms. Since our return to Dublin [from Ulster] one John Fullerton has arrived, who presented himself before us as agent for Sir James Dowglasse, who informed us that he brought fifteen families with him to plant upon the land, with artificers and workmen. A pretty castle upon the pass of the Moyrye, built in the time of the late Earl of Devonshire's [Lord Mountjoy's] Government here, at the Queen's charge; where Captain Anthony Smith is constable, and has a ward of twelve men; has drawn some families of British to dwell upon the lands thereunto adjoining, which is a good relief to passengers between Dundalke and the Newrye."

The first and largest undertaker on the foregoing list was Sir James Dowglasse, one of the King's servants, whose native place was Spott, in Haddingtonshire, and who went to England with James I. on his accession to the English Throne in 1603. Dowglasse became popular in the Royal household, and soon got several substantial pickings in addition to his wages as a servant. He got, by Royal grant, the fines levied from many Roman Catholic gentlemen for "recusancy," or, in other words, for refusing to attend the services of the English Church. This grant of extensive lands in the Fewes was conferred on Dowglasse simply that he might be able to realise a round sum by the sale of it, for few, if any, of the King's servants who had obtained grants in Ulster ever cared to leave their comfortable quarters in the Royal palaces of England. Accordingly Dowglasse sold his estate in the Fewes, known as Clancarney, to Sir Archibald Acheson, in May, 1611, very soon after he had taken out his patent. 2. Henry Acheson came from Edinburgh, and got the proportion called Coolemalish, which was created a manor of the same name. This planter was soon obliged, from failing health, to return to Scotland, and he never appears to have revisited Ulster again. He bequeathed his lands in the Fewes to his brother, Sir Archibald, whose lands of Clancarney adjoined Coolmalish. These brothers were involved in frequent litigation with the Primate and Dean of Armagh, who claimed portions of their property as belonging to the Church. The Achesons, however, were generally successful in these lawsuits, although in one they were the plaintiffs and in another the defendants. 3. Sir James Craig was a servant in the Royal household, coming also from Scotland with the King in 1603, but it is not known to what district north of the Tweed he originally belonged. He was clerk of the wardrobe, and had probably commenced his career as a tailor. He was distinguished, however, by several marks of the Royal favour, including the dignity of knighthood, coupled with this grant of lands in the Fewes. His proportion was known as the manor of Magheryentrim. He very soon sold this estate, almost as a matter of course, for he was an attendant in the palace on all grand occasions. The purchaser of his proportion was John Hamilton, a neighbouring planter. 4. William Lawder came from Belhaven, in Scotland, his grant of lands in the Fewes being known as Kilruddan. Lawder sold his property to John Hamilton, December 4, 1614. 5. Claude Hamilton came from a place called Crichnes, and was one of the first undertakers for lands in Ulster to get out his patent; his proportion was known as the manor of Edeneveagh. During the time he held it he had much litigation with Robert Maxwell, Dean of Armagh, respecting several portions of his property claimed as Church land. He sold out, however, to John Hamilton, who got a Crown grant, in 1617, of the several proportions he had purchased in the Fewes, and from whom the place now known as Hamiltonsbawn was originally named. It was afterwards celebrated in one of Dean Swift's most popular poems.

The planters in the Fewes were greatly harassed by woodkerne, who frequented the extensive woods in that barony, and in the adjoining barony of O'Neilan. Cattle-lifting was the principal offence charged against these marauders, and it was sternly punished. The following among other records remain from the spring assizes held at Armagh in the month of March, 1613-1614 :—" Brian O'Mullan and William Allen stole a cow worth £4, the property of Richard Hanley ; guilty ; to be executed. Hugh O'Creggan, of Creena, stole a grey mare worth £6 6s 8d, at Drumullen ;

guilty; to be executed. Lachlin O'Hanlon, of Carricklaghan, stole three cows, value 20s each, on the 10th of December, 1614; guilty; to be executed. Art M'Gillchree and Killese M'Kerney stole a black gelding worth £4, belonging to Patrick Granton, of Drumfergus; guilty; to be executed These culprits were hanged immediately after sentence had been pronounced, the custom, at least in Ulster, then being to put halters on their necks in the dock, and lead them away through the most public streets to the place of execution.

V.

The Commissioners passed from the Fewes into the barony of Orier, now written Orior, and entered the first of those plantation precincts set apart for servitors and natives. In every one of the five counties intended for plantation by English and Scottish undertakers, some barony considered more rugged and unattractive than the others was allotted to such native gentry as had obtained small grants by their compliance or connivance with the Government. The barony of Orior was found to be more suitable for this purpose than any of the other divisions of the County Armagh, although it contained several sweeps of fertile and pleasant lands. These superior districts, however, were scrupulously preserved for a certain number of servitors or military officers, who were admitted to be undertakers as a reward for their services in the war against the Northern Earls. The servitors in each county were thus placed in close proximity to the native grantees, with the object of keeping the latter in strict surveillance—an object which it was supposed military men could more efficiently accomplish than civilians. The servitors had the privilege—refused for a time to the undertakers—of letting their lands to such Irish tenants as had been turned out of their own farms, and had got no small holdings from the Government; and for this privilege the servitors were expected to be specially careful to prevent the natives from molesting the English and Scottish settlers in the other baronies. It would appear, however, that some jealousies had arisen between the servitors and the Scottish planters in the Fewes, and it was reported at headquarters that the former were not sufficiently careful to restrain the natives from occasional intrusion on the Scottish preserves. When this report reached London, the great King was wroth, and instantly ordered that, if any servitors were justly chargeable with negligence in this important matter, they must be sternly dealt with. The King's determination was conveyed to Chichester in the following terms :—"And, because it has been rumoured that some of the servitors there are willing enough to see the undertakers thus discouraged, that they may relinquish their plantation imperfect and quit the country, if you should find any of them to offend in this manner, you are to discharge them of all their commands and entertainment [pay], and hold them incapable of any future preferment. And because the servitors have the special privilege that they may have the natives to inherit their lands, they ought the more carefully to keep them from being offensive to the undertakers by thefts and robberies. And, therefore, if any of the natives shall be apprehended and convicted of such capital offence, justice must be severely executed upon them without any pardon."

Orior had been the territory of the O'Hanlons from a very early date, for they were a fragment of the Clann Colla, a great tribe which held the supreme place in Ulster before the O'Neills were known as a ruling power. At the time of the plantation their chief was Eochaidh or Oghie O'Hanlon, then very old and infirm. His son took an active part in the rising headed by

Sir Cahir O'Dogherty in 1608, but the old chieftain always remained on the side of the Government. He was adjudged, however, to be directly compromised by the fact of his having given his son shelter in his castle at Ballymore or Tandragee, for only one night, during the revolt. Although the old man might have thus been dismissed, according to law, to die in a prison or even on a scaffold, yet Chichester magnanimously proposed to grant him a pension of £80 a year in lieu of his barony of Orior! And a grant for this amount was actually drawn out and offered to the man who had been hereditary standard-bearer in Ulster, and who, as such, had repeatedly carried his banner in the van of the English forces during their conflicts with Irish enemies. In one such conflict, near the Pass of Moyry, he had all but lost his life from a ghastly wound received in this thankless service. But he did not live to draw even one instalment of his pension, for his life was literally crushed out with grief, his grey hair was brought down in sorrow to the grave on hearing that his son's wife, who was a sister of Sir Cahir O'Dogherty, had perished in the woods after having given birth to a child. His son, with several associates, stood out after the defeat and death of O'Dogherty, despite of Chichester's most strenuous efforts to suppress them. Large sums were offered by the Government for their heads, but these young men, mere youths and scions, in several instances, of the native Ulster nobility, each with his desperate little following of swordmen, were able for the space of three years to keep the plantations in a state of jeopardy and terror. At times, when supposed to haunt in some particular forest, they would issue from another to levy their black mail; and when the settlers in the Fewes expected an assault from the dense woods there, the blow was dealt upon those in O'Neilan from the woods of Clanbrazill or Clancann in that district. These hapless outlaws had been rendered desperate by the cruel and unwise policy which would neither pardon them, nor permit them to leave the country, excepting such only as would bring in the heads of certain persons among their kinsmen or associates! As few or none, however, were found to submit on such atrocious terms, and as the very settlers at last petitioned Chichester to "pardon the wood-kerne or permit them to go beyond sea," he was compelled to give way so far as to permit them to go to Sweden, and enlist in the service of Gustavus Adolphus, the Protestant lion of the North—a service, however, which they hated, and from which they deserted at every possible opportunity to enter the armies of his opponents, the Spaniards. It is recorded in a State paper that the military escorts appointed to conduct these young Ulstermen to their several places of embarkation were charged not to pass, if possible, near any of their former homes, from a fear that they should be rendered even more reckless and desperate when gazing on their native fields and homesteads, then in the hands of strangers. Of course this state of affairs in Ulster created a tremendous hubbub in England, but Chichester was able to explain every point smoothly and satisfactorily. Respecting the situation in Armagh, "The reason," said he, in reply to an urgent and angry letter from the King, "why more stealths have been committed upon the undertakers in that county than the rest is that the woody countries of Clancan, Brasilough [Clanbrazil], Killultagh, Kilwarnan [Kilwarlin], the Brentie, the lower part of Orier and Oneilan, which have ever bred kernes, do border upon them [the undertakers]; besides which Oghie Oge O'Hanlon's rebellion left there many a mischievous knave unpardoned, whom I have now at the instance of the undertakers taken in, and given them his Majesty's pardon, and I pray God it may make them honest." In this case he wanted to lay the blame on the woods, but his own wicked policy did more to "breed kernes" than all the woods in Ulster.

This commotion was in full swing when the Commissioners commenced their measurements and markings-off in Orier. The barony is now divided into Upper and Lower Orier. The upper division contains about 45,397 statute acres, and comprises the whole of the parish of Jonesborough, with part of the parishes of Forkhill, Killevy, Loughgilly, and Belleek. Its only town is part of Newry, and its principal villages are Forkhill, Jonesborough, and Belleek. In this division of the barony the surface is rough and mountainous, and here are Slieve Cullen and the Newry Mountains, with all their spurs and slopes. Lower Orier contains 32,535 acres, and comprises the whole of the parish of Ballymore, with part of the parishes of Forkhill, Kilcloony. Killevy, Kilmore, and Loughgilly. Its towns are Tanderagee and part of Poyntzpass, and its principal villages are Acton and Mountnorris. The surface of Lower Orier is undulating and beautiful, with a fertile soil. In this plantation precinct, including both the divisions aforesaid, the Commissioners found 15,500 arable acres, which were marked off into twelve proportions—two great, three middle, and seven small. These twelve proportions were afterwards distributed among certain servitors, whose names were Sir Gerald Moore, Knight; Sir Oliver St. John, Knight; Lord Audley, Sir Thomas Williams, Knight; John Bourchier, Esq.; Francis Cooke, Esq.; Charles Poyntz, Esq.; Marmaduke Whitechurch, Esq.; and Captain Henry Adderton.

When these servitors were in possession of their several proportions for a year, Sir George Carew made the following report:—"Lord Audley, 2,000 acres, in reversion of Arte MacBarron, and 500 acres in possession as servitor; the 500 acres set out, but no preparation for building. Sir Oliver St. John, Knight, 1,500 acres, as servitor; is making preparations for building. Sir Gerrott Moore, Knight,

1,000 acres, as servitor; has left the most part to Captain Anthony Smith, who has promised to perform the conditions required. Sir John Bourchier, Knight, and Captain Francis Cooke, 1,000 acres apiece, as servitors; Sir John Bourchier is providing materials for building. Lieutenant Charles Poyntz, 200 acres, as servitor; has provided timber and materials for the buildings. Arte MacBarron, of that country, has removed with tenants to lands allotted in Oryer. Carbery M'Cann, chief of his name, has sold his portion in Oryer, and is removed to Clandeboy, where he has lands of Conn O'Neale. The fort of Mountnorris is a good fort, well rampierd, with bulwarks, and a palisade, and a fair deep ditch; within this fort Captain Anderton has built a fair cagework house, and others to keep victual and munition in; some inhabitants of English and Irish, who have settled themselves, have built good houses after the manner of the Pale, which is a great relief and comfort for passengers between the Newry and Armagh; it is a place of special import upon all occasions of service, and fit to be maintained. The servitors being charged by us with backwardness in having done so little, answered for the most part that they had not taken out their patents until the end of Candlemas term last, and that by reason the British [Scottish] do yet retain natives who ought to be their [the servitors] tenants, they are disabled to put things forward as otherwise they would, but they will go roundly in hand with their works this next spring, as they have promised us."

VI.

The first on the foregoing list of servitors, named variously Gerrot, Garrett, and Gerald Moore, was son of Sir Edward Moore, of Mellifont, near Drogheda, who had come from Kent during the war against the Northern Earls, and had been very successful as a soldier of fortune. His son Gerald or Gerrot added very much to the accumulations his father had left. He had specially asked that his proportion as servitor might be allotted to him in the barony of Orier, and his lands, known as Knockduff, appear to have been carefully selected, containing enough but not too much wood and bog. In Pynnar's survey this proportion was known as Ballymonehan, and afterwards as Drumbanagher. 2. Sir Oliver St. John was the second son of Nicholas St. John, a Wiltshire gentleman. He served in Flanders for a time, and was sent to this country in 1601, where he soon rose to much distinction, and eventually became Lord Deputy, although he greatly disapproved of the plantation scheme. He recommended that no English or Scotch should be brought to Ulster, but that the lands ought rather to be let from the Crown to the native inhabitants, thus securing their loyalty and prosperity *in sæcula sæculorum*. His land in Orier included the castle and demesne of old Sir Oghie O'Hanlon, but St. John added other proportions to his estate as they were offered for sale in the district. His grant here conveyed the lands known as the Manor of Ballymore, *alias* Tanderagee. His representative at the present day is the Duke of Manchester. 3. Lord Audley's name was George Tuchet, afterwards Earl of Castlehaven, but he was not a success either as a planter or a politician. Being father-in-law of Davys, the Attorney-General, Audley was able to secure several grants in Ulster, and he appears to have been given 500 acres in Orier as a sort of *sop* to compensate for the short delay he might have to endure before getting possession of Arte MacBaron's 2,000 acres. He had not long to wait. The 500 acres, and indeed the 2,000 also, eventually formed part of the Tanderagee property. 4. Sir Thomas Williams was classed among "servitors not in pay, but willing to undertake." It is not known whence he came, but because of his long services in Ireland the Council in London recommended him warmly to Chichester. He soon sold his proportion, called Mullaghglasse, to Captain Anthony Smith. The fifth name on the list was that of John Bourchier, son of Sir George Bourchier, who had been Master of the Ordnance in Ireland before the appointment of Sir Oliver St. John. Captain John Bourchier was classed among such "servitors as were willing to undertake with some helps and encouragements." His proportion of Tawnavalting was afterwards known as Claire, and became the property of his younger brother, Henry, who succeeded to the Earldom of Bath. 6. Francis Cooke came from Norwich. His proportion, known as the Manor of Balliclare, lay in Orieryetragh, or Upper Orier, adjoining that of Sir Oliver St. John. Cooke also sold his lands to the latter, and settled afterwards in Tyrone. 7. Charles Poyntz was the younger son of Sir Charles Poyntz, of Ironacton, in Gloucestershire. He became an active and influential planter, adding considerably to his Manor of Brennoge, and eventually getting a re-grant of his lands as the Manor of Acton, the name by which the estate is still known. He married Christian Whitechurch, sister to a lawyer who held a proportion adjoining Acton. His son, Sir Toby Poynts, left two daughters, Sarah and Christian. Sarah married Charles Stewart, of Ballintoy, in the County of Antrim, and Christian became the wife of Roger Hall, of Narrow Water. The estate, which was equally divided between these ladies, included a small fragment of 200 acres which Pynnar calls Curiator — a mistake for Oriereightra, Upper Orier. 8. Marmaduke Whitechurch was a successful attorney, whose small grant of Ballymacdermot was soon augmented, and in addition to his property in Orier he had grants of lands in other districts.

9. Henry Adderton, or Atherton, obtained this grant in virtue of his position as keeper or constable of the Fort of Mountnorris. These servitors, as Carew states, complained against the undertakers for delaying the natives on their several proportions, contrary to the conditions, and thus preventing them from coming as tenants to their, the servitors', lands. The servitors had the same complaints to make in every other county, for without the assistance of the natives they could not move in making any improvements, whilst the undertakers would not permit the natives to be removed from them until the first season's crops could be got planted. To meet this difficulty the Commissioners issued a warrant to delay the removal of the Irish for a time, so as not to inconvenience the undertakers "If the undertakers," as stated in the warrant, "are not prepared to manure and till the land against next year, so that if the Irish tenants be presently removed a general dearth is like to follow in those parts, to the prejudice of the plantation—the Irish who now possess the land may hold the same till May next, paying rent for that time [from November, 1610, until May, 1611], to the undertakers, who on their side are to pay the Irish for the corn and fallows when they shall leave their possessions unto them."

In the grant of 500 acres to Lord Audley it is stated that "he is promised 2,000 acres in this precinct of Orier at the death of Arte MacBaron O'Neill, and his wife, both of whom are now [1609] very old and infirm." This old couple were alive in 1611, but they both died soon afterwards, and their removal from their own cherished home at Loughgall very likely hastened their departure from what had become, to them, a very troublesome world. In granting their lands in reversion, Chichester had determined that none of their children, nor children's children, should inherit. Against one of these children—Alice O'Neill—he must have had a rather decided grudge. She had married, as has been said, Conn O'Neill, of Castlereagh, an unmanageable sort of man, who had a facility for getting into dangerous scrapes. Among other freaks he joined the Northern Earls in the war against the Government, but surrendered soon afterwards and got reinstated as a reward for his prompt submission. He was not content, however, to get his head quietly out of the noose, but must celebrate his restoration by festivities becoming an Irish lord. So, as a preliminary, wine was ordered from Spain, and on its arrival at the then little landing-place at the mouth of the Lagan, he ordered its removal to Greycastle [Castlereagh] The servants sent on this mission returned crestfallen, confounded —and without the wine. They stated that certain persons at the port held the wine until they could get paid some overcharge; and when they [the servants] attempted to take it by force they were driven off and very greatly abused. The Lord of Southern Clannaboy and the Ards was furious, and in his wrath he sent a force more than enough to carry off the wine in triumph—not knowing that what he believed to be an overcharge was a duty then recently put upon wines, or that the persons who held his wine-casks were revenue officers, then also quite recently brought to Belfast. But he had done the deed—he had levied war against the King—he had been thus guilty of high treason, and was shut up in a dungeon at Carrickfergus without delay. He was to await his trial for a capital offence; he would not have had long to wait, and his trial at that crisis, and under all the circumstances, could only have had one result. But he was rescued by the heroic devotion of his wife, who, first having made many preliminary and most difficult arrangements for assistance, next found an entrance to his dungeon, releasing him with her own hands and at the most imminent peril of her own life. Our honest old Presbyterian chronicler, the Rev. Andrew Stewart, has recorded several important facts connected with this case, but did not evidently care to be too demonstrative in his admiration of Alice O'Neill's fearless devotedness to her husband. He speaks of her as a "nimble woman," but if he had ventured to describe her as a noble woman his narrative would have lost nothing of its quaint dignity.

O'Neill was no sooner outside the dungeon than Patrick and Thomas Montgomery, two kinsmen to the laird of Braidstane, got hold of him, and carried or accompanied him first of all to Donaghadee, where he was hidden in an old church for a day; and at night, Thomas Montgomery, a mariner, got him on board his own vessel, and quickly brought him across the channel to Largs. From thence Conn was escorted in triumph to the residence of Hugh Montgomery, in the parish of Beith, "where," says the writer of the Montgomery Manuscripts, "he was joyously and courteously received by the laird and his lady, with their nearest friends. He was kindly entertained and treated with due deference to his birth and quality, and observed with great respect by the laird's children and servants, they being taught so to behave themselves." O'Neill and Montgomery then and there agreed to divide the lands of Southern Clannaboy and the Great Ards—the Little Ards belonged to the Savages—into two equal parts, each taking a half, but Conn engaging to convey liberal portions of his own half to Patrick and Thomas Montgomery, in return for the immense services rendered by them in the affair of his rescue. The original document recording this first agreement was destroyed, as we learn from the Montgomery Manuscripts, when Rosemount or Greyabbey House was burned in 1695. Conn O'Neill's devoted wife survived him, and remarried with Henry Savage, of Ard Keen, in the Ards. Her youngest brother, Owen Roe, had gone to the Continent, when a mere boy, where he afterwards greatly distinguished himself as a soldier. He was invited to return in 1642, to command the armies of the Confederated Catholics, which he did with consummate skill, inflicting a great defeat on the Scottish General, Monro, at Benburb. A renegade named Plunket was hired to assassinate Owen Roe, which he did by poison, boasting of his foul deed afterwards. O'Neill felt himself very ill in the camp, near Limavady, and was carried to Cloughonter Castle, the residence of his sister, Mrs. O Reilly, where he soon afterwards died."

Besides Arte MacBarron there were only thirty-eight other natives in the whole County of Armagh who got small patches of freehold in the rugged and sterile barony of Upper Orior. These persons are all designated in their several grants as "gentlemen," and belonged to the respectable native classes throughout the county, but very few of them were able to retain their former standing when removed from their homes and deprived of the lands on which they had pastured their cattle. The surnames that prevailed most among these natives, removed from various districts of the county, and placed in Upper Orior, were O'Hanlon, MacAna or M'Cann, O'Neill, O'Hagan, O'Mellon, and Macdonnell. This policy of placing such native grantees by themselves, and so as that they could be most easily guarded or watched, was adopted solely on Chichester's suggestion. In a document forwarded by him to the Council in London, and headed "Certain Considerations Touching the Plantation of the Escheated Lands in Ulster," the Deputy discourses thus:—"It is very difficult and dangerous to remove and transplant such a number of barbarous and warlike people into any parts of the kingdom; besides that the other provinces are too well acquainted with their lives and conditions, and will be as unapt to receive them. Therefore, the remedy, I conceive, will be to appoint them some one part of the plainest land of their own country; or to intermix their townreeds with ours in plain countries, where they may be environed with seas, strongholds, and powerful men to overstay them, and to proportion those lands indifferently upon meet rents and conditions to keep them in subjection, and that with such equality in the partition, that the contentment of the greater number may overweigh the displeasure and dissatisfaction of the smaller number of better blood" [or higher rank].

But what of the multitudes who got no grants, however small or insignificant? They were utterly cast out, not transplanted; but the servitors and bishops were permitted to take as many of them as they could accommodate, and these hapless natives were greatly preferred as tenants to the English or Scottish settlers of the same class. But, unfortunately, there could not be found room for all on the lands of the servitors and bishops, so that many were scattered over the other provinces, as hewers of wood and drawers of water, who had lived comfortably on their own lands in Ulster amidst their flocks and herds. When it was announced that the bishops and servitors could take Irish tenants, it so happened that many who had got small grants but had good supplies of cattle, surrendered their grants to the Government, and hastened away more quickly than the Government could have wished to rent more extensive lands from bishops or servitors. Those who were slow or too late in thinking of this, foolishly clinging to the hope that they might yet be permitted to retain their own homes, were obliged at last to sell such cattle as their small patches could not accommodate at ruinously low prices. Prominently among those natives who threw back their shreds of land to the Government were the septs of the O'Quinns and O'Hagans. They had followed their creaghting, though not to the neglect of their crops, throughout various districts of Tyrone and Armagh. From the close of the war in 1602 until the escape of the Northern Earls in 1607, the two septs above named had evidently been amongst the leading cultivaters of the soil in their own districts, and with what success we shall here permit one of their exterminators to certify. Sir Thomas Phillips, on hearing of the flight of O'Neill and Tirconnell, made an excursion from Coleraine along the wooded ways of Loughinsholin as far as Dungannon. In a letter to Salisbury, of September 22, 1607, he refers to this journey, and expresses his surprise at witnessing the very prosperous agricultural condition of that district so soon after the close of the desolating war. "I thought good," says he, "for securing of the people to go from Coleraine as far as Dungannon, and going through the country the people met me, and were all amazed and ready to forsake their houses. They now begin to grow rich, so that for the most part during peace they increase very fast in cattle, and this year they have great plenty of corn. I have passed through the fastest [most inaccessible to English troops] country in Tyrone, where I did not expect to see so much corn."

The Government was rather taken aback by this move on the part of many most respectable natives, who preferred having landlords over them to the possession of small freeholds from the King. Davys pretended not to feel any surprise at this, and sought to explain their conduct by the following statement, which may be described as the very reverse of the truth:—"All the Irish, the chief Lords excepted, desire naturally to be followers, and cannot live without a master, and for the most part they love every master alike, so he be present to protect and defend them. And, therefore, I am of opinion that if they were once settled under the bishops, or others who may receive Irish tenants, they would follow them as willingly, and rest as well contented under their wings, as young pheasants do under the wings of a home hen, though she be not their natural mother; and though the transplantation be distasteful to them, as all changes and innovations are at first unpleasant, yet we hope that when they are once seated in their new habitations, they will like the new soil, as well as prove better themselves, like some trees which bear but harsh and sour fruit in the place where they naturally grow, but, being transplanted and removed, like the ground better, and yield pleasanter and sweeter fruit than they did before." The foregoing extract is part of a letter addressed to Salisbury, in September, 1610, and Davys was evidently proud of this figure of speech about the fruit trees, for he introduces it again in another letter to Salisbury written only a few weeks after. In this second letter he states how he had actually told the Irish of Ulster that the King, in ordering their removal from their houses and lands, had "thus imitated the skilful husbandman, who doth remove his fruit trees, not with a purpose to destroy them, but that they may bear better and sweeter fruit after the transplantation." Surely this was heaping insult on injury with a vengeance! But, after all this man's affected nonchalance, he could not help returning again to the fact that the Irish of Ulster, even in that the day of their direst visitation, retained their buoyancy and independence of spirit. In May, 1611, he wrote once more to Salisbury as follows:—"Whereas, it was doubted that the natives in this month of May, which was the time fixed for their removing, would not have been transplanted but with some difficulty, it has fallen out, contrary to their [the Government's] expectation, that they [the natives] are more willing to leave the British undertakers' lands than the British undertakers are to leave them."

COUNTY OF TYRONE.

I.

Tyrone is occasionally spoken of as the premier county of Ulster because it is the largest and most central fragment of that region which formed the ancient principality of the O'Neills. In more modern days that great portion of our Northern province has been curtailed in almost all its boundaries, but the present county still contains the seat of its early government, and is associated more intimately than any of the other counties in Ulster with the history and traditions of the great family above named. In the year 1584 that portion of the principality which lies south of the Blackwater was shired off, and became the County of Armagh; and in the year following another great fragment lying between the Bann and the Foyle was also shired off, and was subsequently known, at least for a time, as the County of Coleraine. At a later period, or in 1608, a third large and very valuable fragment, known as the barony of Loughinsholin, was taken from what had been the principality, and added to the County of Coleraine to form the present County of Londonderry. But still the remaining part of the principality, now known as the County of Tyrone, is of very ample dimensions—something over thirty eight miles in length, from the town of Caledon, on the Blackwater, to the Mountain of Croagh, a little eastward from the Pass or Gap of Barnesmore; and not less than thirty miles broad along its western border, by Strabane and Loughderg. This vast sweep of territory contains 467,175 Irish acres, or 751,387 acres of English measure. These figures may be perhaps somewhat under the mark, if it be a fact, as we have seen stated, that the county contains 450,286 arable acres English measure, 311,867 acres uncultivated, 11,981 acres under wood, and the remainder water, excepting small portions around several country townes.

When the Commissioners of Plantation reached Tyrone from Armagh, they found that it contained four large baronies, named respectively Dungannon, Clogher, Omagh, and Strabane. These have been since sub divided, so as to make eight modern baronies. The Commissioners adopted the old baronial divisions as their plantation precincts, excepting in the case of Dungannon, which, because of its great extent, they divided, naming the lower or northern portion the precinct of Mountjoy. They found that all the lands in Tyrone belonged to the Crown, excepting the Church lands, and excepting about 5,000 acres lying on the western side of the Blackwater, which had been granted by Queen Elizabeth to Sir Henry Oge O'Neill, and were then held by his heirs. These lands comprised the ancient Irish territory known as Mointerburn, and were the inheritance of Sir Felim Roe O'Neill, who resided at Kinaird, on the Blackwater. The termon and herenagh lands in Tyrone, although originally belonging to the early Irish Church, were found by the Commissioners to have been virtually in the hands of the minor septs, *i. e.* of the clansmen, for many centuries, and, such being the case, they fell to the Crown, as all lands held by the people were confiscated by the attainder of the Earl of Tyrone. The barony of Clogher was the recognised territory or "country" of Sir Cormac O'Neill, a younger brother of the Earl, but there is not a word in any of the Commissioners' reports to indicate what had become of him, or on what plea they had appropriated his lands. It was taken for granted no doubt that Sir Cormac held his estates by grant from the Earl, and that the attainder of the latter was enough, as forfeiting all the lands of his tenants as well as those held immediately by himself. When the Earl unexpectedly left Ulster—an event which the Government pretended to regard as deeply offensive, although it was exactly what they wished and wanted—no one was more surprised or upset than Sir Cormac, and he was the very first to bring intelligence of it to Chichester. Sir Cormac had been living on peaceable terms with the Government since the close of the war in 1602; so much so indeed that the Earl does not appear to have given him any intimation of his own intended movements; but Chichester and Davys suspected Sir Cormac of complicity with the Earl, so that when he hastened to Dublin to let them know of the flight from Lough Swilly he was seized, and soon afterwards sent off to the Tower in London, where he pined a woeworn captive for the space of eighteen years, until death released him.

However, during the movements of these Commissioners throughout Ulster an incident occurred which must have reminded them very unpleasantly of the way in which they had dealt with Sir Cormac O'Neill. As they journeyed from Lifford so Enniskillen the Lord Chief Justice Winch, who was of the party, became seriously ill, and was sent by Chichester to recuperate at the residence of Sir Edward Blaney, near Monaghan. On the way thither Winch informs us that he "was in his travel enforced to Sir Cormac M'Baron's house, now prisoner in the Tower." In other words, he was obliged to take refuge for a time in the Castle of Agher. "His lady," continues Winch, "gave us house room, but had neither bread, drink, meat, nor linen to welcome us, yet kindly helped us to two or three muttons from her tenants." This lady was a daughter of the chief house of the O'Donnells, of Donegal, and would probably have been offered a little patch of her husband's lands on plantation conditions, but she died soon after Winch's enforced visit. She had already, however, been doomed to feel and see the Commissioners at work around her, for they commenced with the barony of Clogher during their work in Tyrone. This barony contains 97,569 acres, and comprises part of the parishes of Aghalurcher, Donagheavy, and Errigal Trough, with the whole of the parishes of Clogher and Errigal-Keerogue. Its chief towns and villages are Clogher, Agher, Ballygawley, and Fintona. The Commissioners found in this barony or precinct of Clogher only 12,500 acres of arable land, which they marked off into ten proportions—seven small, one middle, and two great. These proportions were soon afterwards allotted to the following eight English undertakers, viz.:—Sir Thomas Ridgeway, Knight; John Leigh, gentleman; Walter and Thomas Edney, Esqrs.; George Ridgeway, gentleman; William Parsons, Esq.; William Turvin, gentleman; Edward Kingswell, Esq.; and William Glegge, gentleman.

When the above-namd planters had been in possession of their several estates in Clogher for a year, Sir George Carew made the following report of their progress:—"Sir Thomas Ridgeway, vice-treasurer and treasurer of wars in Ireland, 2,000 acres; has appeared in person; his agent is Emmanuel Ley, resident this twelvemonth, who is to be made a freeholder under him; Sir Thomas brought from London and Devonshire, the 4th May, 1610, twelve carpenters, mostly with wives and families, who have since been resident, employed in felling timber, brought by Patrick M'Kenna, of Trugh, County Monaghan, none being in any part of the barony of Clogher, or elsewhere near him—viz., 700 trees, 400 boards and planks, besides a quantity of stone, timber for tenements, with timber ready for setting up a water-mill; he is erecting a wardable castle and houses, to be finished about the next spring; ten masons work upon the castle, and two smiths; one Mr. Farefax, Mr. Laughton, Robert Williams, Henry Holland, and three of said carpenters, are to be made freeholders; other families are resident, wherewith he will perform all things answerable to his covenants. Edward Kingswell, 2,000 acres, has appeared at Dublin and taken possession personally; returned into England to bring over his wife and family; his agent, William Roules, has money imprested for providing materials to set forward all necessary works. Sir Francis Willoughby, Knight [who sold out to John Leigh], 2,000 acres; has taken possession personally; William Roules and Emanuel Ley, in his absence, employed in providing materials for buildings; 200 trees felled and squared. George Ridgeway, 1,000 acres; took possession in person; his agent is resident since March last; some materials ready to place; intends to go forward with building his bawne; some freeholders and tenants to inhabit, but no work done. William Parsons, the King's surveyor, 1,000 acres; took possession personally; his brother, Fenton Parsons, his agent, is resident since March last; has provided materials for building; has two carpenters and a mason, and expects four Englishmen, with their families, to come over shortly; no work done. William Clegge, 2,000; has not appeared, nor any for him; it is reported he passed his land to Sir Anthony Cope, whose son came to see the same, and returned into England; nothing done; by letter he desires to be excused, promising to go on thoroughly with his plantation next spring. Captain Walter Edney, 1,500 acres; took possession personally; his son-in-law resident since March last; provision made for building a house, the foundation laid; six families of English in the kingdom that will come to plant and settle next spring. William Turvin, 1,000 acres; took possession in person; his brother resident since March last; has provided materials for building; agreed with four families to come out of England the next spring to plant, who promised to bring other five families; intends to go shortly in hand with building a bawne and a house, but nothing done yet."

The progress of these planters during the first year may seem slow ; but their difficulties at the commencement must have been serious, and their purses generally were but light 1. Sir Thomas Ridgeway exchanged his proportion of Portclare and Ballykirgir in 1622 for the title and dignity of an earldom. Sir James Erskine came to Ulster, bringing with him from James I. the power of creating an earl, and this power he was permitted to utilise as best he could. He appears to have been fortunate in meeting a ready customer, for the exchange was very simply and speedily made, Ridgeway becoming thenceforth Earl of Londonderry, and Sir James Erskine the owner of the lands in Clogher that had been granted to the former. 2. John Leigh was an engineer by profession, and came to Ulster with the Earl of Essex in 1572. Before the time of the Plantation he had visited many localities in this province as an engineer, and knew many of its leading Irish inhabitants. He appears to have bought the proportion of Fintona from Sir Francis Willoughby even before the latter had taken out a patent, for the grant was made in Leigh's own name. The engineer seems to have had no particular taste for planting, for, instead of bringing strangers on his lands, he let them off to the Irish occupants at the risk of being forfeited for so doing. At his death he was succeeded by his nephew, Sir Arthur Leigh, who sold the estate to Captain James Mervin, or Mervyn. 3. Walter and Thomas Edney, who were brothers, came to Ireland as servitors during the war against the Northern earls, and were generally employed as spies. Walter had received such rigorous treatment as a spy in Spain that he died about 1610; and Thomas was classed among such servitors as "would be content to undertake, but not to build, castles unless by extraordinary helps and encouragements" Both the brothers, however, had soon disappeared, and their proportion of Ballyloughmaguiffe was known for some time as the Manor of Ridgeway, and eventually as the Manor of Blessingbourne, having passed through many hands. 4. George Ridgeway came from Devonshire, and was a younger brother of Sir Thomas. He ranked amongst such servitors as "undertook of themselves, with some help and encouragement," obtaining the proportion oi Ballymakell, which adjoined his brother's lands at Augher, and which he named the Manor of Thomas Court, probably in honour of his brother.

II.

The next or fifth undertaker on the foregoing list was William Parsons, who came to Ulster very poor, and quickly became known as a clever but unscrupulous adventurer. He was the nephew of Sir Geoffry Fenton, another adventurer similarly endowed, and by whose influence Parsons climbed the ladder lightly until he became surveyor-general. He had then ample opportunities for accumulation, which he never, by any chance, appears to have neglected. His proportion of Ballaclogh he named Cecil Manor, in honour of his great patron, the Earl of Salisbury; this name still survives in Clogher as the designation of a respectable residence on the northern frontier of the barony. 6. William Turvin came to take formal possession of his lands, but it is not known from what locality in England he came. He was probably a servant in the Royal service, as he soon disposed of his proportion called Moyenner to Sir Gerrard Lowther. In 1628 this estate had become the property of Archibald Hamilton. 7. Edward Kingswell was, no doubt, a servant in some department of the Royal household, and he appears to have been specially indulged in his plantation business. He did not take out a patent until 1613, four years after the time appointed by proclamation for so doing. He then obtained two proportions, named Ballinconnolly and Ballyranill, both of which he sold in 1616. Sir William Stewart was the purchaser of all Kingswell's lands. 8. William Clegge was another servant of the King, but it is not known from what place he originally came. He sold his proportion, known as the manor of Derrybard and Killaney, to Sir Anthony Cope, so early as 1611. The last mentioned was the same undertaker whom we have already met in the barony of Oneilan.

From Clogher the Commissioners passed into the barony of Omagh, which has, in more modern days, been divided into east and west. The two divisions contain 224,647 statute acres, and include part of the parishes of Cappagh, Donaghcavy, Magheracross, and Termonmaguirk, with the whole parishes of Cloghherney, Dromore, Drumragh, Kilskerry, East Longfield, West Longfield, Skirt of Urney and Ardstraw, and Termonamungan. The principal towns and villages in the barony are Omagh, Baragh, Sheskinore, Dromore, Trillick, Drumquinn, Castlederg, and Sixmilecross. In all this vast precinct the Commissioners only found 11,000 acres arable, which they marked off into nine proportions—one great, two middle, and six small. These proportions were soon afterwards distributed amongst the following English undertakers—viz., George Tuchet, Lord Audley, and Elizabeth, his wife; Sir Marvin, or Mervyn, Tuchet, Knight; Sir Ferdinand Tuchet, Knight; Edward Blunt, Esq.; and Sir John Davys, Attorney-General. Sir George Carew reported of this family party after twelve months' occupancy as follows:—"The Lord Audley, 3,000 acres; has not appeared, nor any for him; nothing done. Sir Marvin Audley, Knight, 2,000 acres; the like, *i.e.*, nothing done. Sir Ferdinand Audley, Knight, 2,000 acres; the like. Sir John Davys, Knight, 2,000 acres; possession taken by his agent, William Bradley, resident, who is preparing materials for building a stone house or castle, with a bawne, which materials will be ready before Allhallowtide next; at this instant the walls of the castle are twenty-two foot high, and in breadth between the walls nineteen foot, and in length thirty-six foot. Already four fee farmers and a carpenter, with their families, are ready to be estated on portions, which they could not receive until now, for that five quarters of the best of the said lands were in controversy, and some of it not yet cleared. The said Sir John intends to finish his works next spring, and to plant and people his lands according to the articles. The Lord Audley and Mr. Blunte came out of England since our return from the North, and went to see their proportions. The Fort of Omey is a good fort, fairly walled with lime and stone, about thirty foot high above the ground, with a parapet, the river on one side and a large deep ditch about the rest, within which is built a fair house of timber after the English manner. All begun by Captain Edmon Leigh, and finished by his brothers John and Daniel Leigh, at their own charges, upon the lands of the Abbey of Omey, at which place are many families of Irish and English, who have built them good dwelling-houses, which is a safety and comfort for passengers between Dongannon and the Liffer. The fort is a place of good import upon all occasions of service, and fit to be maintained."

It thus appears that the barony of Omagh was handed over to a family party, consisting of Lord and Lady Audley, with their two sons and their two sons-in-law, for Blunte and Davys had married Lord Audley's two daughters. Here was surely a gratifying spectacle for the King, who specially rejoiced to see people of rank coming forward to assist him in the grand emprise. "We intend nothing," exclaimed the Scottish Solomon, "with greater earnestness than that the plantation of Ulster, now in hand, with civil men, and men well-affected in religion, should be accomplished." Two special pleas, urged by the King for prompt and vigorous action on the part of his influential subjects, were—that other countries in Europe were watching to discover what this movement in Ulster might really mean, and political critics everywhere were ready to make capital out of any or every failure of the work in hand—or, as he expressed it, "both in respect that foreign States do cast their eyes upon us, and the ill-affected at home and abroad will be ready to take advantage of anything omitted or neglected therein." But his Majesty might have urged another very touching plea on his loyal subjects—to wit, that he fondly hoped the plantation in Ulster might prove the speedy means of relieving him from many importunate people who would get "proportions" as payments, and whose claims of various kinds he did not then see exactly how he could otherwise meet. This aristocratic lot thus launched on Omagh did but little to recommend the project on which their Sovereign has so set his heart. 1. Lord Audley had come from Aditheley or Audley, in Staffordshire, and was the eighteenth Baron Tuchet. He had entirely failed as a planter in Munster, and when the plantation movement was about to commence in Ulster he came hastily northward, and commenced to prowl about this province in all directions in search of desirable localities—a recreation in which he was chiefly guided by his amiable son-in-law, Davys, who had already had many favourable opportunities of taking lessons in Northern topography. First of all, Lord Audley proposed to undertake for 100,000 acres in Tyrone, but in offering for so much he probably intended to accommodate, and to be assisted by, the whole family party above-named. He was ridiculed for asking so much, but he and the other members of his family got 11,000 arable acres, and this with the proportionable extent of unprofitable lands would comprise nearly, if not altogether, the acreage for which he had asked. His 3,000 acres in Omagh included 2,000 for himself and 1,000 for his wife Elizabeth, who was the daughter of Sir James Mervyn, of Fontbill, in Wiltshire. Lord Audley was created Earl of Castlehaven in 1616, but only lived a few months afterwards. He does not appear to have built a castle, and died at an out-of-the-way place called Drumquinn. His Countess soon remarried with Sir Pierce Crosby. His two proportions called Fynagh and Rarone were created the manor of Aeley. When this property was sold after his death, it was found that, besides the original 3,000 in the grant, it contained also 3,000 acres of meadow, 3,000 acres of pasture land, 2,000 acres of wood, 2,000 acres covered with bramble and furze—briars and whins—and 200 acres of bogg, all of which had been thrown in gratuitously to his proportion as waste or unprofitable lands. This account of what was called unprofitable lands on Lord Audley's property was applicable, more or less, to every proportion granted throughout Ulster.

The second name on this family list was that of Sir Mervyn Tuchet, whom Carew, as above quoted, calls Audley, erroneously supposing the latter to be the family name, whereas it was only the family title. His proportion called the Brade was known as the manor of Stowey. Sir Mervyn Tuchet became Lord Audley and Earl of Castlehaven at his father's death. He settled on his Omagh estate, and at the time of Pynnar's inspection, 1618-20, he held not only his own proportion, but that of his younger brother, called Fintonagh, and also that of Blunte, his brother-in-law, known as the manor of Ardleston. He was twice married, first to Elizabeth, daughter of Benedict Barnham, a London alderman; secondly to Anne, daughter of Ferdinand Earl of Derby, and widow of Grey Bridges, Lord Chandos. There was no house of family residence on any one of the three proportions in his possession. Pynnar reported on this planter's estates as follows:— "The agent for the Earl showed me the rent-roll of all the tenants that are on these three proportions; but their tenures are so weak and uncertain that they are all leaving the land. These were in number 64; and each of these hold 60 acres, which they term a town-land. The rest of the land is let to twenty Irish gentlemen, which is contrary to the articles of plantation; and these Irish gentlemen have under them, as I was informed by the gentlemen and tenants in the country, about 3,000 souls of all sorts." 3. Sir Ferdinand Tuchet, the younger son of Lord Audley, married the widow of Sir John Rodney, of Pilton, in the County of Somerset. His proportion of Fintonagh, "the green fields," comprised a part of the ancient Irish territory so-called, as did also the proportion of John Leigh, in the adjoining barony of Clogher, already mentioned. Sir Ferdinand's proportion was known as the manor of Tuchet. 4. Edward Blunte was a native of Harleston, in Derbyshire, and had married Anne, eldest daughter of old Lord Audley. His two proportions of Eddergoule and Carn-acken were known as the manor of Ardleston—probably a misprint for Harleston—the name of Blunte's English estate. 5. Sir John Davys was by birth a Welshman, and married Elinor, third daughter of Lord Audley. Davys's two proportions in Omagh contained 1,000 acres each, and were named Clonaghmore and Gravelagh. His wife remarried with Sir Archibald Douglas, and his only daughter, Lucy, married Lord Hastings, afterwards Earl of Huntington. When Davys supposed that he had done his work in Ireland, and was certain that he had accumulated enormously during his sojourn of seven years in this land, he began to press and petition urgently for permission to return to England. He died in 1626. His work, whilst in Ireland, he describes in general terms, as follows:—

"The escheated lands in Ulster are settled in the Crown, the pretended titles of the natives cleared, the records entitling his Majesty thereto made perfect, and returned, and put into a place of safety. All the English Lords and degenerate English have made surrenders of their lands, and taken back estates thereof, to hold the same according to the course of the laws of England. All the old corporations have renewed their charters, and divers new corporations are erected, to the increase of trade and handicraft within the kingdom." Davys always treated the old Earl of Tyrone's misfortunes with insolent levity—seeing no doubt how much this demeanour pleased the Attorney's employers. In O'Neill's final remonstrances addressed to the King, he describes Davys as "a man more fit to be a stageplayer than a counsel to his Highness." Davys always appeared to O'Neill as if acting a part at the Council table in Dublin. Whether the former was theatrically disposed we cannot say, but that he was an ardent lover of dancing is certain, for he took the trouble of writing a lengthened poem in praise of that popular exercise. The poem was known as "The Orchestra," and was dedicated to Charles I. when Prince of Wales, whom Davys therein designates as "the fairest flower of noble chivalry." As the young Prince was a good dancer, the poet could not overlook this fact in his dedication :—

Then dancing's praise may be presented well
To him whose actions add more praise thereto
Than all the muses with their pens can do.

III.

From Omagh the Commissioners passed onward to the barony of Strabane which Chichester had some difficulty in clearing out for plantation. This barony had formed, in the olden time, an Irish territory occupied by a powerful and numerous sept known as the Clann-Arte O'Neill, or descendants of an Arthur O'Neill who lived at the commencement of the fifteenth century. His representative towards the close of the following century was the gallant and well known Neal Connelagh O'Neill, who had succeeded in uniting two rival sections of the clan, and had thus become a power in the North-West of Ulster. His two chief residences were old, strong castles, or rather fortresses, at Strabane and Newton, now Newtonstewart. Neal Connelagh desired, generally, to maintain peaceable relations with the English, and his successors adopted the same policy. His grandson, Turlough, surnamed Luinech, because he was fostered in a family of the O'Looneys, fought fiercely on the side of the English against his kinsman Shane O'Neill; and Turlough's son, Arthur or Arte, as fiercely opposed Hugh, the Earl of Tyrone. This Arthur O'Neill left four sons, all of whom gave their services regularly to the Government, and expected, and were led to expect, that, as a matter of course, they would be permitted to inherit the lands and residences enjoyed for many centuries by their ancestors. But at the close of the war against the Northern earls, and after the suppression of O'Dogherty's insurrection, the Government began to feel that it need no longer depend for assistance on native septs, and that the urgency of the plantation movement would not permit the claims of these four brothers to be recognised. They were permitted, it is true, to hold small grants of land at different places and on plantation conditions; but the old patrimonial lands held, time immemorial, by their ancestors as heads of the Clann-Arte, was cut up into new divisions and distributed among a lot of Scottish undertakers.

In the meantime, however, and before the plantation movement had actually commenced, Chichester had taken it on himself to grant a custodiam of the two castles at Newton and

Strabane, with the demesnes belonging thereto. In his "Notes of Remembrances" the Deputy made the following entry :—"I have delivered the possession of the Newtowne, with some three Ballybetaghs of land [about 3,000 acres], to Tirlagh and Neal M'Arte, the children of Sir Arte O'Neale, in respect of the good services they did against the traitor O'Dogherty, and the relief they gave to the Liffer upon the burning of Derry. I think this sufficient for them, but they do not. If the King will be pleased to reserve the town of Strabane, which stands within the lands now assigned to them, and give them a greater scope on the other side, I think it would be best for his service; for divers Scottishmen will plant there, and make it a pretty town, albeit it was all burned to the ground by O'Dogherty, which was the cause they [the young O'Neills] were permitted to take it at this time." The brothers made as good a fight as they could for better terms, and Tirlagh, the eldest of the four, undertook the risk and expense of a trip to London, that he might lay their case personally before the Council, but without materially changing the decision already made. He brought back a letter from the Council to Chichester, containing their final answer, as follows :—"We recommend the bearer, Tyrloghe O'Neale, eldest son of Sir Arthur O'Neale, Knight, for two middle proportions [3,000 acres] in the precinct of Dungannon, in Tyrone. He besought us for all the land in Ulster called Slewsheese [about 11,000 acres] which formerly belonged to Neal Connelagh O'Neal, his great grandfather. Of these lands he only has a custody grant from you of the castles of Strabane and Newtowne, with some ballybetaghs of land belonging to them. He now prays that he may have in addition to the two proportions we have recommended for him the castles of Benburb and Knockicligh, in the barony of Dungannon, but this we leave altogether to your judgment, as to you is left the placing of the natives. Considering his acceptable services, and his willingness to be transplanted, we hope he may be extraordinarily respected in the greatness of his proportion, and in the choice of a good seat for his greater comfort. One other middle proportion should be divided among the other three sons of Sir Arthur O'Neale, namely, Neal, Con, and Bryan." Slewsheese was the then local name at Strabane of the great range now known as the Sperrin Mountains, extending from that barony to within four miles of Garvagh, a reach of about thirty-six miles.

Tirlagh O'Neill and his three brothers were obliged to be satisfied to be removed into the barony of Dungannon, although Chichester refused to allow them the possession of the two old castles there which they appear to have wished for. The Commissioners had thus free access to all the barony of Strabane, which is very extensive, containing 240,490 statute acres. In this precinct, however, they only found 13,500 plantation acres, which they marked off into eleven proportions—one great, three middle, and seven small—distributing them soon afterwards amongst the following Scottish undertakers, viz.:—James Hamilton, Earl of Abercorn; Sir Claude Hamilton, James Clephane, gentleman; Sir Thomas Boyd, Sir George Hamilton, Sir John Drummond, James Haig, gentleman; and George Hamilton, gentleman.

Fully a year after these planters had taken possession of their several proportions, Sir George Carew reported of them as follows:—"The Earl of Abercorn, chief undertaker, has taken possession, resident, with lady and family; has built for the present near the town of Strabane some large timber houses, with a court 116 feet in length and 87 in breadth, the groundsells of oaken timber, and the rest of allor [alder] and birch, which is well thatched with heath and finished; has built a great brewhouse outside his court forty-six foot long and twenty five foot wide. His followers and tenants have since May last [1611] built twenty-eight houses of fair copies; and before May, his tenants, who are all Scottishmen, built thirty-two houses of like goodness. He is preparing materials for building a fair castle and bawne, which he means to put in hand for the next spring. There are 120 cows in stock for his own use. Sir Thomas Boyd, Knight, has a proportion of land; is resident with his wife and family, and is providing materials for building. Sir George Hamilton, Knight, has a proportion of land, and resident, with his wife and family. He has built a good house of timber for the present, sixty-two foot long and thirty foot wide. He has brought over some families of Scots, who have built themselves a bawne and good timber houses, eighty cows and sixteen garrons among them. Sir John Drummond, Knight, appeared in person, took possession, and has one Scottishman, two garrons, and a mare. James Clapham [Clephane], 1,000 acres; resident, prepares to people his land, and has a competent store of arms in readiness. James Hayge or Haig, 1,500 acres; has not appeared, nor any for him; nothing done. Sir Claude Hamilton, Knight, 2,000 acres; has not appeared, nor any for him; nothing done. George Hamilton, 1,000 acres; he has taken possession, is resident, and making provision for building."

Thus, the precinct of Strabane was invaded by a distinguished family party from Scotland, for the planters there were all kinsmen variously related, excepting two or three who were servants of the King. In this particular, the Hamiltons in Strabane were circumstanced similarly with the Audley party in the adjoining barony of Omagh, except that the two sets of undertakers belong to different nationalities. Jealousies appear to have sprung up between them at an early period originating probably in the fact that the King was specially pleased by

Hamiltonian zeal in the plantation, although it could not be said to exceed that of the Audleyan party in the same direction. But such was the Royal anxiety for Abercorn's success that on the 7th of May, 1611, James wrote to Chichester "requiring him to take out of all the companies in Ulster in his Majesty's pay, and out of all the wards there, the number of twenty-five footmen to attend the Earl of Abercorn, for his aid in the plantation." This kingly care for Abercorn seems to have rendered him too exacting, and rather prone to take offence for trivial causes. On one occasion a dispute arose between him and Lord Audley about a small portion of debatable land on their mutual border; and Lord Abercorn, like a petted child, thought proper to complain to the king that, in the course of their controversy on the question of mearings, Audley had said something slightingly of the whole Scottish nation! The King, being a Scotchman himself, was gravely offended, and even gave expression to his displeasure. Fortunately for Audley, he had an influential advocate in his son-in-law, Sir John Davys, who wrote to the Earl of Somerset, a member of the English Council, as follows:—"Part of this barren land borders on the barony of Strabane, where the Earl of Abercorn is the principal undertaker, by occasion whereof there grew a controversy touching a small piece of land. Some ill intelligence was carried between their noblemen by servants or undertenants, as it ever falls out when there is a difference between such persons of quality. Among other things it was reported that Lord Audelay had let fall some unfit speeches against the Scottish nation in general, and this was not only told the Earl, but also the King, and the King was pleased to let the Lord Deputy and myself to know as much. My Lord Audelay being afterwards advertised that the King takes notice thereof, and being grieved that such a report should be made of him, has written this enclosed letter to me, wherein he makes protestation of his innocence in that behalf, and desires that the same might be made known to some of his honourable friends in England, who might acquaint the King therewith, otherwise he would come over to England and cast himself at the King's feet, and never leave until the King is assured of his innocence." Audley's enclosed letter is a rambling account of his own loyalty and old family position, and also of his having been in danger of his life from the Scotchmen in Strabane, although he had as many Scotch as English on his own lands.

IV.

Of the Hamiltons who settled on the lands of Sir Arthur O'Neill's sons in the barony of Strabane certain explanatory notes may be added. 1. James Hamilton, the first Earl of Abercorn, was a grandson of the second Earl of Arran in Scotland, and obtained a grant of lands in the barony of Strabane, including 3,000 acres—one large proportion and one small, named respectively Dunnalong and Strabane. The family residence takes its name of Baronscourt from the court originally erected there of timber and thatched with heather. The two proportions above-mentioned were separated from each other by the proportion of Cloghognall, now incorporated with the Baronscourt estate. 2. Sir Claud Hamilton was the Earl of Abercorn's next brother, and resided in Scotland at a place called Lerleprevicke. He got two small proportions of 1,000 acres each, and known respectively as Killeny and Teadane or Eden. In 1620 Pynnar reported that Sir Claude had died, and that he had left his lands in charge with Sir George Hamilton, his brother. An inquisition held at Augher, in May, 1631, states that these two proportions of Killiney and Eden were held by Sir William Hamilton, probably a son of the original patentee. 3. James Clephane or Clapham had been and then was a servant in the Royal Household; he was one of many in the same class who accompanied the King when coming across the Tweed to be enthroned as Queen Elizabeth's successor. James I. had probably owed this Clephane a round sum, for he borrowed occasionally from his humblest lieges. In December, 1607, there is a grant from the King to Clephane of "the moiety of so much money as is or may be due to the Crown from the statute for purchases of lands at undervalues." In August, 1611, when Clephane was coming to secure a portion of the Ulster spoils, he carried with him a letter from the King to Chichester in the following terms:—"The bearer, James Clapham, goes to Ireland as an undertaker. Inasmuch as he is an old servant whom the King desires to favour, his Majesty has bestowed on him the castle of Newton (now Newtownstewart), in Tyrone, and commands him to be kindly used and furthered in his settling. Grafton, 20th August, in the 8th year of our reign." [1611.] Thus the castle and a large slice of the lands that had been owned during many centuries by the great sept or clann Arte O'Neill was handed over to a servant of the King, as payment, probably, for accumulated arrears of wages. Clephane's grant included two proportions of 1,000 acres each, and named respectively Newton and Lislapp, the whole premises being created the manor of Newtowne. In the proportion of Newtowne stood the historical old castle of Neal Connelagh O'Neill and his ancestors, and in the proportion of Lislapp stood the two great piles known as Castlemoyle and Shancasla, also family residences of the O'Neills, and associated with many striking events in their history.

The associations and traditions of these

grand old family residences, however, were entirely lost on Clephane, their new owner, who only looked at his lands in a thoroughly business-like spirit. It is curious, indeed, that Clephane, who was spoken of by the King as so "faithful," should act so contrary to his Royal master's wishes after leaving his service, for the first and perhaps the only act which he (Clephane) did as an undertaker was to let out his entire lands to Irish tenants, contrary to the conditions of plantation. This simple process (always so highly disapproved of by the King) saved a world of trouble, which the introduction of British tenants incurred, and gave the largest and most satisfactory returns from the lands in the shape of rents. Clephane was no doubt thwarted in his policy, but at all events he very soon sold his estate to Sir Robt. Newcomen, who was in possession at the time of Pynnar's survey (1618), and who rebuilt the old castle of the O'Neills at Newtowne. Sir Robert Newcomen resold this property to Sir William Stewart. On the 26th of July, 1629, letters patent of denization were issued to Sir William Stewart, and also a grant unto him of four several proportions—namely, the two small proportions of Ballyneconnolly and Ballyravill, in the barony of Clogher, and the two small proportions of Newtowne and Lislapp, in the barony of Strabane, and other lands, amounting to 140 acres, lying in the barony of Strabane. The two proportions of Ballyneconnolly and Ballyravill are created into a manor, to be called the manor of Mount Stewart; and the other two proportions of Newtowne and Lislapp are created into a manor, to be called the manor of New Stewardstown [Newtownstewart]. Sir William Stewart's grandson—William Montgomery of the "Manuscripts"—passed a few years of his boyhood at Newton, and has left the following account of his hurried departure thence at the time of the outbreak of the insurrection in 1641 :—"I was kept at school in Newtown-Stewart house, and had a pike and a musket made to my size; and on the 23rd of October, 1641, I was in the garden performing the postures of my arms, my grandfather, Sir William Stewart's foot company, himself viewing his soldiers and their arms, and exercising them, when about foure hours afternoon, to our amazement, a man half stripped came with a letter signifying the insurrections, murthers, and burnings on all sides committed by the Irish. The messengers, one after another, came sweating and out of breath from divers quarters, with like consternation and haste as Job's escaped servants did to tell him of his losses; and they related the cruel massacres of divers persons. Sir William, leaving a guard in his said house, went next morning with his lady and family, to Strabane, and thence to Londonderry, ten miles further."

The remaining planters in the barony of Strabane are also worthy of brief separate notices. 4. Sir Thomas Boyd, who got a middle proportion known as the Manor of Sheane, was brother in-law to the Earl of Abercorn, the latter having married Sir Thomas Boyd's sister Marion. Sir Thomas Boyd was son of the fifteenth representative chief of the Boyd tribe or clan in Kilmarnock, and was known as of Bedlay and Bonshawe. He married Grissel Cunningham, a granddaughter of the fifth Earl of Glencairn. His father, the fifth Lord Boyd, had made himself notorious in the clan feuds and fights of his own district, but he suffered from some malady which made him more known as an invalid than any exploits he had been able to perform as a clan warrior. In 1597 he got a pass from the King (then James VI. of Scotland) to travel in foreign countries for his health, and of this Royal document the following is a copy:—

"We, understanding that our cousing, Thomas Master of Boyd, is vexed with ane grievous dolor in his heid, and other diseises in his body as that he cannot find sufficient ease and remeid within our realme, but is in mind to seek the same in foreign countries where the same may be maist convenientlie had, thairfor givis and grantis licence to him to depart and pass forth our realme to the partes of France, Flanders, Well of the Spa, and other partes, where he pleisis, there to remaine." With what results this trip was attended does not appear, but it is known that this old gentleman's son was amongst the very first Scottish undertakers in Ulster to secure his patent for his proportion of Sheane, which lay on the border of County Donegal, from which it was separated by the River Finn. It is probable, however, he was soon called on to succeed his father at Kilmarnock, for he disposed of his Ulster lands to the Earl of Abercorn, and is not mentioned afterwards as having lot or part in the plantation. 5. Sir George Hamilton was third brother of the Earl of Abercorn, and was known as of Greenlaw, in Scotland. He got the middle proportion of Largie or Cloghognall, and the small proportion of Dirreowen, which lay along the River Derg, and was somewhat distant from the former. There is no mention of this planter or his lands in the printed inquisitions of Ulster, and his estate is now also a part of the Baronscourt property. Sir George Hamilton incurred the displeasure of the King by becoming a recusant and a Roman Catholic, and his services were, therefore, no longer wanted as an Ulster planter. His grandson, General Richard Hamilton, led the army which Lord Tyrconnell sent against the Northern Protestants in 1689. 6. Sir John Drummond came from Menteith, and was one of a great Perth family, all the members of which, in their generations, were devoted adherents of the Stuart dynasty. His proportion of Ballymagrieth lay near the town of Omagh, from which it was only separated by a little stream, the boundary line between the two baronies of Omagh and Strabane. Sir John does not appear to have been a popular landlord, for Pynnar reports that, "although there are many tenants on his lands, they have no estates [tenures] at all; insomuch that they, knowing I was in the country, came and complained unto me, and said that for these many years they could never get anything from him but promises; and, therefore, the most part of them are leaving the land. I desired the lady to show me their counterpaines, but her answer was that her Knight was in Scotland, and that she could not come unto them; but upon examination, I found there were 30 men of Brittons [from Scotland] on the land." Sir John Drummond was styled as of the Rosses, in the parish of Capprey, where he died in May, 1625. He left no children, and his brother Malcolm succeeded to the estate. The latter got a re-grant of the premises, which were created into a manor, to be called the manor of Castle Dormand. 7. James Haige came from, or rather belonged to, some Scottish district, but he appears not to have even visited his proportion of Meenterlong. He was a servant of the King, and became a political agent or spy on the Continent. He soon disposed of his lands to Sir William Stewart and Sir George Hamilton. In 1629, Sir Henry Tichbourne got a grant of the greater part of Haige's proportion, his lands being created a manor called the manor of Mounthill —so named, perhaps, from the mountainous nature of the surface. 8. George Hamilton, gent., who got the small proportion of Teadane or Eden, came from Bynning, in Scotland, and was a kinsman of the other Hamiltons who planted in the same barony. He, in common with the Hamiltons generally, was descended from Sir Gilbert de Hamiltown, who is said to be the founder of this numerous tribe or race. This George Hamilton of Bynning belonged to the well-known family seated at Fingaltown, in Renfrewshire, and was the thirteenth in descent from Sir Gilbert above-mentioned. George Hamilton was son of Sir John Hamilton, his mother being a daughter of Sir Thomas Otterburn, of Redhall. He had served in the army of Gustavus Adolphus, and on his return from Sweden he appears to have been attracted to Ulster for a time; but he soon sold his lands to Sir Claude Hamilton, although he had taken possession, and had made some preparations for building. His proportion of Eden lay on boundaries of the baronies of Coleraine and Loughinsholin, being intersected by the tail or termination of the great range known as the Sperrin Mountains. The River Derg flows through this proportion from end to end. This estate, with that of Killiney, was, in 1629, granted to Sir William Hamilton, the lands being created a manor, to be called the manor of Ellistown.

V.

The plantation precinct named Mountjoy comprised the northern or lower division of the barony of Dungannon, and was set apart for the accommodation of seven Scottish undertakers. It was so called from a fort in the district, and the fort when being built had been named in honour of Lord Mountjoy — the general who, by bringing fresh relays of soldiers from England, was able to defeat the worn-out and wasted forces of the Northern earls, in 1602. Although the name was used in plantation documents for a few years, it appears to have been discontinued after 1620, and the old one resumed for the whole barony. Indeed, the surveyors of 1609 did not call this precinct Mountjoy, but wrote it down on their map as "Parte of the barony of Donganon." This great barony is since divided into upper, middle, and lower, and is bounded on the north by the County of Londonderry, on the east by Lough Neagh and the lower part of the Blackwater, which separate it from the Counties of

Antrim, Down, and Armagh ; on the south by the upper part of the Blackwater, which separates it from the County of Monaghan, and on the west by the baronies of Clogher, Omagh, and Strabane. In this precinct of Mountjoy, the surveyors could only find 10,500 acres of arable land, although it really contained about 50,000 statute acres—all of which was thrown in gratuitously with the 10,500 arable acres to the seven undertakers placed thereon.

The names of these undertakers were as fowlow : — Andrew Stewart, Lord O'Chiltree ; Robert Sewart, of Hilton, gent. ; Sir Robert Hepburne, Knight ; George Crayford or Crawford, Laird of Lochnorris ; Bernard Lindsey, gent. ; Robert Lindsey, gent. ; and Robert Stewart, of Rotton, Esq. Of these Scottish planters in the precinct of Mountjoy, Carew makes the following report in 1611, or a year after they had taken out their patents :—Lord Uchelrie, 3,000 acres ; being stayed by contrary winds in Scotland, arrived in Ireland (at the time of our being in Armagh, upon our return home), accompanied with 33 followers, gents. of sort [gentlemen of rank], a minister, some tenants, freeholders, and artificers, unto whom he hath passed estates ; he hath built for his present use three houses of oak timber—one of 50 feet long and 22 feet wide, and two of 40 feet long, within an old fort, about which he is building a bawne. There are two ploughs going on his demesne, with some fifty cows and three score young heifers landed at Island Magy [Magee], in Clandeboy, which are coming to his proportion, with some twelve working mares. Sir Robert Hepburne, Knight, 1,500 acres; sowed oats and barley the last year upon his land, and reaped this harvest forty hogsheads of corn ; is resident ; hath 140 cows, young and old, and eight mares ; is building a stone house forty feet long and twenty feet wide, already a storey high ; intends to have it three stories high, and to cover it, and the next spring to add another storey to it; good store of timber felled and squared, and providing materials to finish the work. The Laird Lochnorris, 1,000 acres; being deceased himself, as we are informed, had his agent here, Robert O'Rorke; hath timber felled, and is preparing materials for building against the spring. Bernard Lindsey and Robert Lindsey, 1,000 acres apiece; have taken possession personally in the summer, 1610, returned into Scotland; agent, Robert Cowties, resident; a timber house is built on Robert Lindsey's proportion; hath eight mares, and eight cows with their calves, and five oxen, with swine and other small cattle, and a competent portion of arms. Robert Stewart, of Haulton, 1,000 acres; hath appeared in person and brought some people; timber felled, and preparing materials for building. Robert Stewart, of Robstone, 1,000 acres; hath appeared in person, with tenants and cattle; timber felled and squared, and providing materials for building. The castle of Mountjoy, upon Lough Chichester [Lough Neagh], beside the old fort, wherein are many inhabitants both English and Irish, together with Sir Francis Roe's foot company. Here is a fair castle of stone and brick, covered with slate and tile, begun in the late Queen's time, and finished by his Majesty. It is compassed about by a good strong rampier of earth, well ditched, and flanked with bulwarks. In this castle Sir Francis Roe, the constable, and his family dwell."

These Scottish planters had got into a desirable locality, and they appear generally to have commenced with vigour. 1. Andrew Stewart was the fourth Lord Ochiltree, and was descended, through the Stewarts of Avondale, from Murdock, Duke of Albany. One of this family exchanged the barony of Avondale for that of Ochiltree with Sir James Hamilton, of Finnart, about the year 1534. This fourth Lord Ochiltree had become embarrassed, and was obliged to sell his barony of Ochiltree with other family property, the title passing away with the barony to the purchaser, who was Sir James Stewart, of Killeth. Although, therefore, this undertaker was by courtesy styled Lord Ochiltree in his Ulster patent, he was only plain Andrew Stewart; but as an encouragement to him and his son, and to reconcile them to their two proportions of Revelinowtra and Revelineightra, the King conferred upon the young gentleman the title and dignity of Earl of Castlestewart. The father died in March, 1639, and was succeeded in all his landed property by his son. In 1629 the father had got a re-grant of three proportions in the precinct of Mountjoy, created into the two manors of Castlestewart and Foreward. 2. Robert Stewart, of Hilton, or Halltown, was described as an indweller in Edinburgh, and was the first of the Stewart family here who settled at Killymoon, near Cookstown. He purchased the lands in his proportion from Sir Francis Cooke, before getting a grant of them from the Crown; and a younger brother also obtained a grant of the proportion of Gortville, or Gortegal, in the same district. The grant to the older brother contained the two Irish territories of Ballyokavan and Ballyoquinn, or all the lands in the district of the present Cookstown. 3. Sir Robert Hepburne was a member of the well-known Aulderstown family of this name. In 1605, this undertaker of the middle proportion of O'Carragan was a lieutenant of the King's Guard, and in this capacity was sent to the Western Isles of Scotland to receive surrenders of the castles of Dunyveg and Dowart. He was also commissioned on that occasion to prevent the escape of any rebellious Islesmen, by seizing their boats. This undertaker is called Haybourne by Pynnar, and he was styled as of Killaman, in the County of Tyrone. He had parted with his proportion before 1629, as in that year there is a grant of it from the Crown to Henry Stewart. 4. George

Crayford, or Crawford, belonged to a family in Cumnock, Ayrshire, a branch of the Crawfords of Loudan. Lefuories or Lochnorris Castle stood on the Lugar, not far from Cumnock, but the Crawford estates there eventually passed into the possession of the Earls of Dumfries, who superseded the old castle by a fine residdence known as Dumfries House. George Crawford died soon after getting his grant in Tyrone, and in the time of Pynnar his lands were owned by a Captain Sanderson. 5. Bernard Lindsay and Robert Lindsay were sons of Thomas Lindsay, of Kingswork, Leith, although the former came to Ulster from Lough Hill, in the County of Haddington. Bernard sold his lands soon after getting possession, and in Pynnar's time his proportion of Craigballey was owned by Alexander Richardson. Robert Lindsay remained in Tullahoge, near Dungannon, and was the founder of a respectable family there. 6. Robert Stewart, of Rotton, or Robstone, or more correctly Robertstown, was uncle of Andrew Stewart, Lord Ochiltree, but he does not appear to have done more than take possession of his proportion of Ballenkenan, which, in the time of Pynnar, belonged to Lord Ochiltree's son. 7. The brother of Robert Stewart, of Hilton, or Halltown, aforesaid, sold his proportion of Gorteville or Gortegall soon after getting possession, and in the time of Pynnar it was owned by David Kennedy. These Stewarts, "indwellers in Edinburgh," and the two Lindsays were all servants or caterers in some fashion to the King.

The remaining, and much the more extensive part of the great region known as the barony of Dungannon, was allotted to certain leading servitors and a few natives who had been deemed worthy of some recognition by the Government. The three sections into which this barony is now divided when taken together, extend twenty-two miles from east to west, and about the same length from north to south. These three divisions, although separately dealt with as three baronies, are represented on the ordnance survey maps as if undivided; and it is to be observed that they only form one barony in the old survey of 1591, which was made by the Government at the urgent request of the great Earl of Tyrone. The vast region anciently, and in modern times, known as Dungannon contained the three Irish territories of Magh-Lomchlair, which lay around Donaghmore; Ui Briuin, now Minterburn, in Aghaloo; and Ui Caracain, or O'Caraghan, now comprised in the parish of Killaman. This barony is so extensive as to include almost all the varieties of surface in Tyrone, containing rich meadow lands along the flat sweeps adjoining the shores of Lough Neagh; fertile grain-bearing undulations on the banks of the Blackwater; and dismally bleak uplands in some other localities. The area of the whole three divisions comprises something more than 216,000 statute acres. This area contains part of the parishes of Arboe, Artrea, Ballinderry, Clonfeacle, Derryloran, Killyman, Lissan, and Tamlaght, together with the whole parishes of Aughloe, Ballyclog, Carranteel, Clonoe, Desertcreaght, Donaghenry, Donaghmore, Drumglass, Kildross, Killishall, Pomeroy, and Tullynaiskin. The chief towns are Dungannon, Caledon, Aughnacloy, Moy, Cookstown, and Stewartstown; and the chief villages are Pomeroy, Coalisland, Grange, Carnteel, Tullyhoge, Castlecaulfield, Donaghmore, Coagh, and Newmills.

The inhabitants of this barony adhered unflinchingly to the Earl of Tyrone, as a general rule, until his final separation from them in the autumn of 1607, when he sailed from Lough Swilly never to return. The inhabitants of Dungannon were exceptional in their fidelity, for long previously to his "Flight" many of his own name and kindred had fallen from their allegiance to The O'Neill, and had even learned to take up and circulate every evil report concerning him. Among the Carew MSS. is a paper drawn up by a well-known servitor named John Leigh, who was high sheriff of Tyrone in 1608, and who kept what he called a "Breefe of some thinge which I have observed in the several baronies of the County of Tyrone." Amongst other matters, "I observed," says he, "that there are certain kindreds or septs of the Neales [O'Neills] in divers parts of Tyrone, which ever did, and still doe, as much as in them lyeth, oppose both against Tyrone [the Earl] and all those of his proper sept and party—namely, in the barony of Strabane, Tirloghe, Oge O'Neale, son to Sir Arthur O'Neale, and all his followers and dependents as well of the Neales as of the Quinns, and likewise of divers other septs on that [the Strabane] side of the Slewsheese. Alsoe in the barony of O'Meaghe [Omagh] all that sept of the Neales called the Clan-Arte doe deadly hate Tyrone and his septs. And likewise in the barony of Clougher are two other distincte septs of the Neales, who hate Tyrone and his septs—one of which septs are the sons of Shan O'Neale, and their followers."

VI.

The surveyors of 1609 could only find 16,000 arable acres in the precinct or barony of Dungannon, not including of course the 9,500 arable acres already noticed in the precinct of Mountjoy. Remembering, however, the vast extent of the Dungannon precinct, and making due allowance for church lands and educational grants, and grants to certain forts therein, it will be seen that the planters had ample room for expansion here, as in all the other escheated baronies, because of the vast sweeps of what were termed unprofitable lands being thrown gratuitously into their several proportions.

The Plantation Commissioners marked off the precinct of Dungannon into twelve proportions —two great ones of 2,000 acres each, four middle-sized of 1,500 acres each, and six small ones of 1,000 each. These were allotted to eight servitors and four natives, whose names are as follow:—Sir Arthur Chichester, the Lord Deputy; Sir Thomas Ridgeway, Treasurer at War; Sir Richard Wingfield, Knight, Marshal of the Army; Sir Toby Caulfield, Knight; Sir Francis Roe, Knight; Francis Annesley, Wm. Parsons, Tirlagh O'Neill of Caslane, Esq.; Neal O'Neill, Esq., brother of Tirlagh; Bryan O'Neill, Esq., also a brother of Tirlagh, sons of Sir Arthur of Newton Castle, now Newtownstewart; and Catherine Ny Neill, wife of Tirlagh Oge O'Neill, deceased, and remarried to Robert Hovenden, gent.

The following is Carew's report on the progress made by the above-named servitors at the end of the first year's occupancy of their respective proportions:—"Sir Arthur Chichester, now Lord Deputy, has 600 acres about Dungannon, as a servitor, where he intends to build a castle, or strong house of lime and stone; has masons and workmen to take down such remains of the old castle as are yet standing. There are families of English and other civil men who for the present have built houses of copels, but are bound to build cage-work or stone after the English manner, and make enclosures about the town. Sir Thomas Ridgeway, 2,000 acres, as servitor; hath carpenters providing timber for building next spring. Sir Richard Wingfield, 2,000 acres, as a servitor; has great store of timber for buildings, and will have other materials ready by the beginning of spring. Sir Toby Caulfield, 1,000 acres, as servitor; is making preparations for building. Sir Francis Roe, 1,000 acres, as servitor; is providing materials for building. William Parsons, 1,000 acres, as servitor; preparing to forward buildings next spring. Francis Annesley, 400 acres, as servitor; has made a bawne of earth and sods, with convenient ditch and flankers, and provided timber to build a substantial house within it. Captain Tirlagh O'Neale, one of the natives of Tyrone, has removed, and dwells on his lands in the precinct of Dungannon; has no preparations for building but an Irish house."

It is to be observed that here, as in other baronies allotted to servitors and natives, the former class got the choicest lands, whilst the latter were obliged to accept the rough and comparatively barren portions of the soil. 1. Sir Arthur Chichester had in the first instance 600 acres immediately surrounding Dungannon, which comprised a large section of the demesne lands of the O'Neills, and on it stood their old family residence, mentioned in the Annals of Ireland at the year 1430 as the abode of Owen or John O'Neill, the then Prince of Ulster. It would not now be considered a very princely palace, for, although built of stone and very spacious, it was thatched with heath or heather. It seems to have so continued until the time of Hugh, the great Earl of Tyrone. When the latter married Mable Bagnall in 1593 he had commenced to build "a faire house," as Fynes Moryson informs us, "which," that chronicler further says, "our Government thinks a tye of civilite." In order to cover this fair house in a civilised fashion the Earl procured a vast quantity of lead, but just at that juncture he was hurried into the commencement of the seven years' war with the Government by the undisguised provocations of Fitzwilliam and Bagnall—so the lead, instead of being used for roofing purposes, was converted into bullets. At the battle of the Yellow Ford, on the Blackwater, one of these bullets found its way through Bagnall's brain, and so terminated the career of a very turbulent and cowardly servant of good Queen Bess. However, the remains of O'Neill's old castle were cleared away by Chichester, who had one for himself placed on its site, but the latter has long since disappeared in its turn, although built by Captain Sandford—a crack hand at such work—in the summer of 1618. 2 Of Sir Thomas Ridgeway we have already a brief notice in connection with his two proportions of Ballykirgir and Portclare, in the barony of Clogher. This proportion in Dungannon was originally the Largie, but it was afterwards known as the manor of Ridgeway, the town of Aughnacloy being now the most important place in the district. Sir Thomas Ridgeway was a prominent member of several commissions appointed to carry forward the plantation movement, and to him we are chiefly indebted for the beautiful baronial maps of 1609, representing the six escheated counties of Ulster. 3. Sir Richard Wingfield belonged to the family of this name at Letheringham, in the County of Suffolk, which family is believed to have represented an older branch seated at Wingfield, in the same county, before the Norman Conquest. Sir Richard commenced his Irish career under the auspices of his uncle, Sir William Fitzwilliam, the notoriously money-loving Lord-Deputy, whose three administrations form three of the most disastrous periods in the history of this country. Wingfield was appointed Marshal of Ireland in 1600, and after the close of the war, and the subsequent defeat of O'Dogherty in 1608, he was frequently in Ulster at the head of formidable forces required to keep the Northern Irish in order whilst their lands were being confiscated, surveyed, and set apart for the occupation of strangers. He was created Viscount Powerscourt in 1618, and he died in 1634, his estates devolving upon his cousin, Sir Edward Wingfield, who had served in Ireland during the Viceroyalty of Robert, the second and last Devereux, Earl of Essex. This estate was known as the Manor of Benburb, and lay along the Blackwater, which separated its lands from those in the County of Armagh. The Powerscourt estate has been recently sold to a firm of Belfast whisky manufacturers. 4. Sir Toby Calefield, now written Caulfield, came from Oxford, but not much appears to have been known about his family. However, he served the Queen gallantly, first in Spain, then in the Low Countries, and lastly in Ulster. Amongst the numerous adventurers coming here during the war with the Northern earls, no one, perhaps, was more fortunate than Sir Toby—at least in the accumulation of landed property. After an uninterruptedly-successful run from about 1606 to 1620, he surrendered the various great fragments of his lands, and got out a renewal of the whole in one patent, dated July 12, 1620, so that an indefectable estate in all his lands might remain to him and his heirs in the several counties of Armagh, Tyrone, Monaghan, Derry, Louth, Cavan, Fermanagh, and Donegal. His estates contained every variety of landed property, for he had extensive grants of rich abbey lands, and he had a patent, also, of all the mountains in Ulster, which, being omitted in the survey of 1609, were regarded as concealments in the plantation of this province. He died unmarried in 1627, at the age of 62, and all his gettings went principally to his nephew, the son of Dr. James Caulfield. 5. Sir Francis Roe was the son of Robert Roe, of Lower Layton, in Essex, and grandson of Sir Thomas Roe, Lord Mayor of London in 1568. This Sir Francis—a distinguished servitor in Ulster—was a younger brother of Sir Thomas Roe, the well-known diplomatist, whose first public employment was his mission to the Great Mogul in 1614. In 1607, immediately after the Flight of the Earls, Sir Francis Roe and Sir Tobie Caulfield were appointed governors of the upper or southern part of Tyrone and the whole of the County Armagh. In June, 1616, Sir Francis Roe enfeoffed Sir Garrett Moore, Viscount Drogheda, Sir Roger Jones, Sir Nicholas White, and George White, of Dundalk, as trustees to administer his property for his own use during his life, and afterwards for that of his wife, Margaret Row, or Rowe. 6. Of Sir William Parsons, the surveyor-general of the escheated counties in Ulster, there has been a brief notice in connection with his proportion of Ballenclogh, named by him the Manor of Cecill. We shall hear of him again as a planter in the County of Cavan. 7. Sir Francis Ansley's grant in this precinct is still known as Manor Annesley, and the lord of the manor is bound *in perpetuo* to pay £10 yearly to a school in Clanaghrie—the Irish name of his proportion. Clanaghrie borders on the western margin of Lough Neagh, and is included in the present parish of Clonoe, two miles south-east of Stewartstown. A little river rising in the vicinity of the place last mentioned crosses Clanaghrie in its course to Lough Neagh, and on this stream stands the old Castle of Mountjoy.

Of the natives who chanced to get somewhat liberally of the land-spoil few were able to retain their allotments until the time of Pynnar's inspection in 1618-1620. Of this small number, however, one was Tirlage, the son of Sir Arthur O'Neill, of Newtown and Strabane, who was located near Dungannon, and who had his proportion erected into a manor, and called by the name of Caslane. Another grant which continued for a time was that made to the widow of Tirlagh Oge, son of Sir Henry O'Neill, of Minterburn. This lady was the mother of the well-known Felim Roe O'Neill and several other children, amongst whom the lands thus granted were distributed after the Celtic custom observed in such cases. Although this distribution violated the feudal law of succession so ruthlessly introduced by the Government themselves, yet Chichester was fain to adopt the Celtic law, in this case at least, as being most likely to promote the peace of the district. Accordingly, the Deputy procured a King's letter, or Royal mandate, March, 1612, in the following terms :—" Sir

Henry Oge O'Neill, Knight, lately slain in the King's service against the traitor O'Dogherty, being possessed of lands in the Counties of Tyrone and Armagh, and the King being informed that it would tend to the quiet of those parts if the said lands were divided in some convenient manner among the issue male, you are hereby authorised to accept the surrender of the heir (Felim Roe O'Neill), and to divide the said lands among the issue male of the said Sir Henry as you shall think fit, to be held by each of them, and his heirs for ever, or for such estate and at such rents as you shall think fit. You are also to assure to the wife of the said Sir Henry Oge, and to the wife of his eldest son, deceased, such parcels of the premises during their lives as you shall think fit." Accordingly the two widows, with all the sons and grandsons of Sir Henry Oge, received grants ; but the grantees were to hold by the feudal tenure of knight service, which was an unfair arrangement for them, because being bound by the conditions of plantation, they ought to have had their lands by the more liberal and less expensive tenure of free and common soccage.

There were sixty natives in Tyrone who got small grants, generally of sixty acres each. They were all transplanted into portions of the barony of Dungannon which neither undertakers nor servitors would occupy. These natives are all described in the Government grants as gentlemen, and the surnames most common amongst them were those of O'Neill, O'Hagan, O'Quinn, and O'Donnelaugh, or Donnelly.

About the year 1603, and immediately after the old Earl of Tyrone had been nominally restored to his estates, a proclamation was issued by Sir George Carew, the then Lord Deputy, regulating the "rates for the wages of artificers, labourers, and household servants within the County of Tyrone." From this rather curious and interesting we make paper a few extracts as follow :—

"All manner of persons being under the age of fifty years, not having to the value of £6 sterling of their own proper assets, shall be compelled to labour for their living. No labourers or servants shall depart out of one barony into another without leave of a justice of peace. No person not having the eighth part of a plough shall keep any servant in his house, but shall labour and do his work himself. No person shall hire any servant for less than a year. No servant shall depart from his master without giving a quarter's warning before witness, and at the end of his term the master shall give him a certificate of good behaviour, upon pain of 40s. No person shall harbour or relieve any servant, being departed from his master without certificate, upon pain of 10s. Every plough holder shall have wages by the quarter 6s 8d sterling, with meat and drink. Every leader of the plough shall have by the quarter 5s, with meat and drink. Every beam holder shall have by the quarter 3s 4d, with meat and drink. A good servant maid by the year 10s. A cowboy, for every cow for the half year, 1½d. A cowboy, for two heifers, 1d. Every labourer shall be hired by the day, with meat, 2d. From Michaelmas to our Lady Day in Lent, with a dinner, 2d. Every labourer, without meat, per day, 4d. A master carpenter or mason shall have, per day, with meat and drink, 6d. Without meat and drink, 12d. Every apprentice, being able to work well, 2d. For making a plough beam, with meat, 8d. For the best cow-hide, 5s. For the largest pair of broaghs, 9d. For women's broaghs, 6d. The best plough iron shall be sold for 4s. For making a plough iron, the owner finding iron, 18d. Every smith shall bring axes, spades, shovells, and such necessaries to the common markets. A weaver shall have for every weaver's slatt containing three market slatts, 4d and eight quarts of meal; of 1,000 or 1,600, a meddar of meal and 1d. For weaving a mantle, a meddar or two gallons of meal and 3d. For weaving the best caddowe, a meddar of meal and 4d. For weaving a jerkin, 2d. A cottener, for the best mantle cottened in the best fashion, his dinner and 6d. For cottening the best mantle with cards, his dinner and 6d. For cottening the best caddowe with shears, being the best fashion, 8d. Every one refusing or leaving his work because of these rates is to be fined 40s, or imprisoned until he be content."

COUNTY OF LONDONDERRY.

I.

The present County of Londonderry is a somewhat curious specimen of territorial patchwork, the several fragments of which it is formed being arbitrarily regarded as one, although nature had put some of them distinctly asunder by the intervention of two large rivers. The first and largest fragment once formed a portion of the ancient principality of Ulster, but, being shired off by the English in 1585, it was afterwards known for about a quarter of a century as the County of Coleraine. To this fragment was added another in 1609, which also had been taken from the old principality, and was known as Loughinsholin. Another fragment was added at the same date from the County of Donegal, on the western side of the Foyle; and still another from the County of Antrim, on the eastern side of the Bann. The County of Coleraine was divided into the three small baronies of Coleraine, Limavady, and Anagh, now known as the baronies of Coleraine, Keenaght, and Tirkeeran. The barony of Loughinsholin, subsequently added to the three others above-named, was anciently so-called from Lough-inis O'Lynn, the island of O'Lynn's lake-dwelling—a well-known position near the village of Desert Lynn, now Desertmartin. This barony of Loughinsholin included the two sub-divisions of Glenconkeyn and Killetragh, memorable for their wealth of ancient forests. The fragments taken from the counties of Donegal and Antrim became what are since known as the Liberties of Derry and Coleraine.

The old County of Coleraine, although originally constituting an important part of the O'Neill principality, was recognised from an early date as peculiarly the country of the Ui Cathain, or O'Cahans. This great tribe was a kindred family or race of the O'Neills, and were descended in common with the latter from that Eoghan or Owen from whom the principality of Tyrone took its name. The O'Cahans first appear in Northern history under the tribe name of Fir or Fear-na-Craebh, or "Men of the Creeve," the territory of the Creeve being so-called from the celebrated cataract of Eas Craebhe, afterwards known as the Salmon Leap. At this place, Craebh, a daughter of the prince who occupied the ancient fortress of Dun-da Bheann, now Mount Sandal, was drowned; and hence the ancient Irish name of the waterfall, and also of the territory associated with the earliest history of the O'Cahans. To this district their chieftains, although only vassals of the O'Neills, gradually annexed the whole territory comprising the three baronies of the County of Coleraine, and were ever regarded as the most trusted adherents of the principal house. Towards the close of the sixteenth century the representative of this very long line of chieftains was Donnell Ballagh O'Cahan, who had married a daughter of the Earl of Tyrone, and who, for a time, was the most efficient ally of the latter in the deadly struggle against the Government, commencing in 1595. In the spring of 1600, however, Donnell Ballagh had changed his mind, and on the landing of Sir Henry Docwra at Derry, at the head of a large English force, he surrendered to the Government, and joined Docwra with all the Irish troops under his command, on condition that he should have a grant from the Queen of all the lands which his family had hitherto held under the O'Neills. This condition, with one or two trifling reservations, was then gladly accepted by the Crown, for, in thus securing the defection of O'Cahan, O'Neill's principal support was swept away. O'Cahan was forthwith granted a *custodiam* of his "country" until a regular grant could be made out, and every day from the date of O'Cahan's desertion O'Neill was observed to become weaker until the crisis of his surrender in 1602.

But when O'Cahan had thus efficiently assisted the Government in defeating O'Neill in the field, and afterwards in worrying him at the Council table and in the courts of law, he was unable to obtain his own grant, as had been promised. His lands came in a very short time to be regarded as much more valuable and acceptable than any future services he could ever likely be able to render; and indeed, from less to more, it came out at last that he, Donnell Ballagh, and all the O'Cahan's together, were simply intruders on their own lands from the date of the Act known as the 11th of Elizabeth, which had not been repealed, nor even in any degree modified, and which vested in the Crown all the lands included in the principality of Tyrone. Donnell, to be sure, had been created an English knight, but that fact he felt afforded him but cold comfort under the circumstances. He now also had got the Lord Deputy Chichester to deal with, and the latter was not likely to make allowance for sulkiness on the part of any Irish chieftain, however unfortunate. We had better, however, permit Chichester to explain the situation in his own words:—"The Earl of Tyrone made challenge to this country [O'Cahan's] as passed unto him by letters patent, and required Sir Donnell O'Cahane, the now chief of that name, to give him £200 a year, in consideration of this challenge, but being unable to make him payment of so much, in respect of the waste and riotous expenses otherwise, he yielded one of the baronies up to the Earl in lieu of the £200 which the Earl possessed at the time of his flight; and albeit it is thought that neither Tyrone nor O'Cahane had any good and lawful estate in that country, the right being in the King by the statute 11 Elizabeth, yet it is my duty to declare that the whole country was promised to the said Sir Donnell O'Cahane upon his submission in the year 1601 by the Lord Mountjoy, then lord deputy; and in confirmation hereof a *custodiam* was passed to him under the Great Seal. He is now prisoner in the Castle of Dublin. If he be found unworthy of the King's favour by reason of his treasonable practices and misdemeanours, then is that country in the King's hands to dispose as shall seem best to his Majesty." Unfortunate Donnell! He had begun to regret his conduct towards the Earl of Tyrone, and on hearing that the latter was seen journeying towards Lough Swilly, O'Cahan suspected that he was about leaving Ulster, and determined, at the eleventh hour, to follow and embark with him. But he was too late, although he rode in hot haste, and crossed at several ferries in apparent desperation. O'Neill had sailed, and O'Cahan was seized when he soon afterwards visited Dublin as a "suspect" merely, for the "head and front of his offending" appears to have been his anxiety to make his escape in good company from the turmoils then the order of the day in Ulster. At all events, no pretext for his punishment or even trial could be found, and his longer presence in Ireland being feared to act somehow as a hindrance to the plantation, he was sent to the Tower in London, where he was doomed to suffer a life-long imprisonment. He lingered there from 1609 to 1628, and was only released at last by the kindly interposition of death.

Amidst all the excitement and horror caused at this crisis in Ulster by the violent discussions preparatory to carrying off to the Tower of O'Cahan with Sir Cormac O'Neill and Sir Neal O'Donnell, the Commissioners of plantation went upon their way rejoicing. Having performed their work in Tyrone, they started from Dungannon, journeying still Northward. They wanted to make their way directly to Limavady, then the most conspicuous position in the County of Coleraine, or "O'Cahan's country," but the shortest road lying through the Sperrin and Slievegallon passes was at that time unavailable because of great rains, and the party was thus compelled to take a rather circuitous route through Desert Linn, now Desertmartin, and the woods of Glenconkeyne. "The 24th," says the chronicler of their movements, "we marched towards Coleraine. The mountains of Slewsishe [Sperrin] and Slewgannon [Slievegallon] not being passable with carriages, we were constrained to pass by Desert Linn and Glanconkane, near to Kilulter [Killetragh], the great fastness of Tyrone. Through the glens in this passage we were enforced to camp three nights." In the preceding autumn a lot of Commissioners, with Chichester at their head, took the same route through the woods, "where the wild inhabitants," as Davys then jokingly remarked, "wondered as much to see the King's deputy as the ghosts in Virgil wondered to see Aeneas alive in hell." The barrier then presented by the vast Slewsheese or Sperrin range is not so formidable now, as roads have been since made along the four glens by which it is intersected, one running almost parallel with the mountain range from Newtownstewart to Draperstown, along the picturesque highland defile of Glenelly, which separates the Sperrin range from the Munterlony mountains. Slievegallon is in the parish of Lissan, and nearly four miles north-west from the town of Moneymore. It forms at once the commencement and highest portion of that chain which extends north by west to the sea at Magilligan Point.

The road by Desert Linn, although then leading through a labyrinth of woods and wilds, was level, and had at least one rare attraction for the Commissioners as conducting them to the celebrated lake-dwelling of Loch-inis-O'Lynn, already mentioned, and on which they determined to erect a fort for the protection of the settlers who might be there located. The lake is partly in the townland of Desertmartin, and partly in that of Annagh and

Moneysterlin, the last name being a corruption of Mainister-O'Fhloinn, and derived from a monastery founded there by a chieftain of the O'Lynns. On Sunday, the 27th, the Commissioners emerged from the woods in the neighbourhood of Limavady, for the vast forests of Glenconkeyne and Killetragh stretched down in that direction to the shores of Lough Foyle. The chronicler of the party states that on the day above-named they "obtained [reached] Limavadie, the chief house of O'Cahan, and the best town of that country, and camped a mile and more from the town. The 28th of August being Monday, they began the Assizes and the rest of their business at Limavadie, and ended the Thursday following." On that day, also, Davys snatched from his own peculiar work as much time as enabled him to write to Salisbury. From his letter we make the following extract relative to the several works on hand:—"We are now in the County of Coleraine, which contains O'Chane's fruitful country, and is the third stage in our journey. We pursue our first course in describing and distinguishing the land. Our geography has had the speedier dispatch, inasmuch as here the county is but little, consisting only of three baronies, and as they had sent two surveyors before to perambulate the country, and to prepare the business by gathering notes of the names, sites, and extent of townlands. This they performed well and readily, being accompanied with but a slender guard. I speak of a guard as of a necessary circumstance; for though the country be now quiet, and the heads of greatness gone, yet their geographers do not forget what entertainment the Irish of Tyrconnell gave to a mapmaker, about the end of the late great rebellion; for one Barkeley being appointed by the late Earl of Devonshire to draw a true and perfect map of the north parts of Ulster (the old maps being false and defective), when he came into Tyrconnell the inhabitants took off his head, because they would not have their country discovered."

The concluding portion of this letter relates to the controversy between the Crown and the Church on the Herenagh and Termon lands, and as the Bishops so pertinaciously adhered to their claims, we give Davys's own account of their overthrow in O'Cahan's country:—"For the distinction of Church lands in this country, we had a jury of clerks or scholars ; for the jurors, being fifteen in number, thirteen spake good Latin, and that very readily. These clerks, being chosen in the presence of the Lord Primate, should by reasonable presumption rather be partial for the clergy than for the King. They conceived their verdict or presentment in a singular good form and method, and gave us more light than ever we had before touching the original and estate of Herenaghes and Termon lands. Here at length, after long expectation, the Lord Bishop of Derry [George Montgomery] came to the camp, and was present at the getting up of the jurors' presentment, wherein because it was found that the lands possessed by the Herenaghes and their septs were their proper inheritance, and not the inheritance of the Bishops, and that the Bishops had only rents out of those lands, and not the lands themselves (though herein they concurred with the verdicts given in Tyrone and Armagh this year, and with all the presentments made the last year, being indeed the manifest and infallible truth), yet because it contradicts his Lordship's suggestions made in England with great confidence and assurance, namely, that these lands were the very demesne lands of the Bishops, upon which suggestion his Majesty was speedily moved to confer all those lands to their several sees : therefore, his Lordship took exception to that part of the verdict, affirming that he would not believe that they all agreed in that point ; and therefore he examined them by the poll, before the Lord Deputy and the rest of the Commissioners, and though he expostulated with them somewhat roundly and sharply (which might have altered such poor men as must live under his jurisdiction), yet every one held his opinion constantly, and every one severally gave such plain and probable reasons for his opinions that the Commissioners were fully satisfied, and the presentment was received." The results, therefore, of this inquisition at Limavady respecting the Crown and Church lands were as satisfactory to the Commissioners as those arising from similar investigations at Armagh and Dungannon, and, indeed, as found afterwards in the remaining three counties of Donegal, Fermanagh, and Cavan. All the Herenagh and Termon lands were taken to be temporal lands, and Davys, in his "Abstract of Titles," stated that "there is no part of the temporal lands lying within this county granted to any person, but all remaineth in his Majesty's hands to be disposed of to undertakers, except the moiety of the Royal fishing of the Ban." The half of the Bann fishings belonging to the Crown was between Lough Neagh and the Salmon Leap, which half or moiety the King granted to James Hamilton, assignee of Thomas Ireland. Hamilton by deed assigned and conveyed the same to Sir Arthur Chichester, and the latter was obliged, for valuable considerations, to surrender it to the Londoners soon after having secured it himself.

II.

Whilst Davys and others were thus engaged in clearing the King's title on a point involving extensive territory in each of the six counties, the surveyors and those appointed to mark off the lands in proportions were busy in their several special departments. They commenced work in the barony of Coleraine, which, in remote times, had contained two divisions, North and South, the former being occupied by the great tribe Gaura, and the latter by the sept Donagh. The northern division of this barony was occupied, even at an earlier period, by the Fir Li, a family or race well known in ancient Irish records. The northern half barony of Coleraine was designated in the olden days as Machaire or Maghery, the "Plain," lying between the mountain of Benevenagh or Ben-Albhne and the River Bann The greatest length of this "Plain" is seventeen miles, whilst its breadth varies from two to nine miles. Its northern boundary is the Atlantic; and its southern the barony of Loughinsholin; on the east it is bounded by the County of Antrim; and on the west partly by the barony of Keenaght. The southern part of the barony of Coleraine was the country of the sept Donagh, and lies a little to the north-west of the present town of Kilrea. The whole barony Coleraine, north and south, comprises somewhat over 104,800 statute acres, and contains the present parishes of Agivey, Aghadowey, Desertoghill, Dunboe, Errigal, Killowen, Macosquin, Ballyaghran, and Coleraine, with part of the parishes of Kilrea, Tamlaght-O'Crilly, Balrashane, Ballywillen, Ballymoney, and Kildollagh. In this barony the Commissioners of survey found about 8,000 arable acres, which was marked off into seven proportions—one large, one middle, and five small. The names of these proportions were Boughtbegg, Forntinule, Lisetrim, Claggin, Magheriboy, Cam, and Moycosquin. The last proportion on this list contained 600 acres which had belonged to the ancient and well-known abbey of this name. The proportion called Cam or Camus contained the lands of the celebrated abbey founded by St. Comghall on the Bann, about three miles south of Coleraine.

From the barony of Coleraine the Commissioners passed into that of Limavadie, now Keenaght. This barony, first known as Limavadie—Leim an-Mhadaidh, the "Dog's Leap"—contained the three sub-divisions of Keenaght, Farnacreeve, and Ardmagilligan. Keenaght, which now gives name to the whole barony, is a contracted form of Cianachta, the name of an ancient tribe or clan dwelling there, and expelled by the O'Cahans. Cianachta of Keenaght was the district around the present town of Dungiven. Farancreeve — Feara-na Craebh, "men of the Creeve,"—as already stated, was the earliest tribe name of the O'Cahans, who dwelt originally on the western side of the Bann, in the district opposite the celebrated waterfall of Eas-Creeve, afterwards known as the "Salmon Leap," and now as the "Cutts," near Coleraine. Ardmagilligan, the third old sub-division of this barony, is now known as Magilligan, and was originally so named from a numerous, though never a powerful, tribe, the Ui-Giollogain, who held the whole district from the summit of Benevenagh and the mouth of the River Roe northward, to the east side of the entrance of Lough Foyle, and thence four miles in a south-eastward direction along the Atlantic. This modern barony of Keenaght comprises about 128,692 acres, and contains the parishes of Aghanloo, Balteagh, Bovevagh, Drumachose, Dungiven, Magilligan, and Tamlaghtfinlagan; with part of the parish of Banagher. In Keenaght the Commissioners found 8,000 arable acres, which was marked off into seven proportions—one great, two middle, and four small. The names of these proportions were Dowlinn, Culmore, Cammes, Barcagh, Rousky, Mackan, and Dungiven. The proportion last named contained the lands connected with a castle of the O'Cahans, and with the famous old monastery there in which these chieftains had their principal burying-place.

From the barony of Limavadie or Keenaght the Commissioners moved into that of Annagh, now Tirkeerin. This barony also contained three sub-divisions or sub-territories in ancient times, named respectively Tyrchyrine, Sgryn, and Clandermed. The first of these sub-territories is now represented by the district of Faughanvale, the second by the district of Cumber, and the third by the district of Clondermot. This barony comprises about 102,000 acres, and contains the parishes of Clendermot, Lower Cumber, and Faughanvale, with part of the parishes of Bannagher and Upper Cumber. Tirkeerin was found by the Commissioners to contain only 8,500 arable acres, which were marked off into eight proportions—one great, one middle, and six small. The names of these proportions were respectively Lisglasse, Loyer, Monaghbegg, Moyeghboy, Carnemoyagh, Brackmoy, Kildonan, and Limavadia. Anagh, the place from which the whole barony received its old name, was about two miles to the north-east of Derry. At this point the O'Cahans had a well-known castle or residence, as well as one at Limavady.

After the Commissioners had finished their work in Keenaght, they passed southward into the borony of Loughinsholin. Their map of 1609, prepared soon after their return to Dublin, presents this large barony in two sections, the first containing the ancient territories of Killetragh, Tamlaght, Tarraghter, and Melannagh; the second section containing Glanconkeyne and Clandonnell, the last-named territory being so called as the inheritance of sept descended from a Donnell O'Neill. The first section of the barony is represented on the map as bounded east by Lough Begg and the River Bann, on the south-east by Lough Neagh, on the south-west and north-west by the barony of Dungannon, and on the north by the barony of Strabane. This whole section is also represented as wooded, but free from bogs. The castle of Toome, between Lough Neagh and Lough Begg, is marked on the map as in a ruinous or decayed condition. The second section, containing Glanconkeyne and Clandonnell, is shown on the map as also very much wooded, with several patches of bog in the latter territory around the present Innisrush. The two principal and best known territories in Loughinsholin were Glanconkeyne and Killitragh. The former is called Gleann Concadhain in the Annals of Ireland at the years 1526 and 1584. On Norden's map the name is written "Clanconcan;" and on Speed's map "Glan-kankyne," lying between Slew Gallon and Carntogher. This region, which was so clothed in dense woods, forms the western part of the barony of Loughinsholin. Killetragh-Coill-iochtarach, the lower wood, was separated from Glenconkeyne by the River Moyola.. John Leigh, a very active servitor, in his Briefe already quoted, has the following reference to this district:—"In the barony of the Glynnes, called Loughinsholyn, the inhabitants, consisting chiefly of the Neales [O'Neills], the Haggans, the Mulhallans, with the M'Cahirs and the Quinnes, are wholly those which had their dependence upon the Earl of Tyrone and his sept, and in this place, especially about that part of the barony called Killytraghe, being a strong fastness, do inhabit the chiefe nest of those that, upon any sudden occasion offered them, would first show themselves in action for Tyrone's party, they being able, out of this one quarter, to draw together at least 200 able men, and well-armed, within 24 hours. Also, I have observed that under colour of having liberty to wear arms in the time of O'Dogherty's rebellion, for their own defence, the country is now everywhere full of pikes and other weapons, which their Irish smiths daily make." In Loughinsholin, the Commissioners found 13,500 arable acres, which were marked off into fourteen proportions—two great, one middle, and eleven small. The names of these proportions respectively were—Ballinemanagh, Drumrott, Tirnafessy,

Gortoonra, Ballymacrossy, Moysaden, Oyna, Cohoire, Carramony, Tyrassan, Cully, Ballyvoley, Ballyleitrim, and Lackah.

The Commissioners had now completed their work in Loughinsholin, and in the three other baronies above described, but where were the applicants or undertakers? They had carved up "O'Cahan's fruitful country," as Davys expressed it, and had spread out the land-banquet as invitingly as possible, but where were the hungry speculators and intending planters who had crowded around the Commissioners in other counties? They were conspicuous by their entire and determined absence. There is no trace in the State papers, so far as we know, of any individual applicants for lands either in Loughinsholin, or in "O'Cahan's fruitful country." The doom of that Northern Lord must have shocked the community to some extent both north and south of the Tweed, whilst the planters and speculators generally were afraid that O'Cahan might be permitted to return. There is, or has been hitherto, a sort of affected mystery as to the real origin of the Londoners' plantation—as to whether the scheme was hatched in the Court or in the Corporation. There need be no mystery whatever about it. The King and his councillors, informed no doubt by their Irish agents and emissaries, saw at a glance that no undertakers could be induced to go singly, or even in small companies, to settle between the Bann and the Foyle, and they also knew very well the cause. The Scottish Solomon then became suddenly and deeply impressed with a faith, which he could have had only at second hand, in the great power and resources of the London Corporation, and, being urged on by others, he could not rest until he had enlisted its assistance in the settlement of this otherwise impracticable county. There is no doubt the idea originally arose in the Council or Cabinet, and from that moment the Corporation was sought to be led into the transaction by every possible inducement. On the first quarrel—and there were many—between the two parties, the Corporation in self-defence declared: — "About July, in the 7th year of James [1609], came a proposition by the Lords of the Privy Council to the city of London to undertake the plantation of divers lands of great extent in the province of Ulster, in the remotest parts of the North of Ireland, at that time deserted by other planters, which the City at first refused to undertake; but, upon pressing importunity of the said Lords that some selected persons from the City might be sent to view the country, and that the said plantation might be undertaken, upon the signification of his Majesty's earnest desire to further the said work, and upon tender of large privileges and immunities to invite them thereunto, certain persons of the City [of London] were employed to view the premises."

III.

The Londoners were very hard to be moved, and indeed would not and did not move until they got every point down to the minutest details granted and arranged as they required. The Council wrote to Chichester that the Londoners were then ready and "willing to undertake such a part as might befit them in the project of the plantation of Ulster, and to be a means to reduce that savage and rebellious people to civility, peace, religion, and obedience; and having commissioned the bearers—John Brode, goldsmith; John Monroes, Robert Treswell, painter; and John Rowley, draper, to view the country and make report on the return, you are to direct a supply of all necessaries in their travel in those countries, and to aid them in every way. And we have directed Sir Thomas Phillips to accompany them, whose knowledge and residence in those parts, and good affection to the cause in general, we assure ourselves will be of great use at this time, seeing there is no man that intendeth any plantation or habitation in Ulster who ought not to be most desirous of such neighbours as will bring trade and traffic into the ports." The closing sentence in this letter was a gentle hint to certain servitors, who believed they could secure very comfortable "habitation in Ulster," even if the Londoners were never to show their faces, and who did not relish the idea of having to surrender their lucrative fishings and abbey-lands for the delectation of these London drapers and painters. Not apparently satisfied, however, with sending the foregoing letter by the persons who came to spy the land, the Council, through another channel, on the same day, Aug. 3. 1609, wrote again to Chichester, as follows:—"Referring to our foregoing letter, recommending certain citizens appointed by the city of London to view the Derry and Colrane, and the country between them, we anxiously entreat you to select discreet persons to conduct and accompany them, who shall be able to control whatever discouraging reports may be made to them out of ignorance or malice. The conductors must take care to lead them by the best ways, and to lodge them in their travel where they may, if possible, receive English entertainment in Englishmen's houses. And though we have the opportunity to lay the first hand on this offer and to make the project to the city; yet that it may be well followed up, we send the same in that letter enclosed; and must leave it to you to perfect. The persons sent with these citizens to conduct them must be prepared beforehand to strengthen every part thereof by demonstration, so as they [the citizens] may conceive the commodities to be of good use and profit; on the other hand, that matters of distaste [*mal-apropos* questions], as fears of the Irish, of the soldiers, of cess, and such like be not so much as named, seeing that you know that discipline and order will easily secure them."

It is curious to read these instructions to the Deputy in the light of succeeding events. The English visitors, who were thus only to be lodged in "Englishmen's houses" in O'Cahan's country, must have got an occasional peep, during their peregrinations, into or at Irishmen's houses, too—for only a few months later we find this same Council suggesting that the Irish houses, from which the owners were to be turned adrift, should be preserved for the use of English settlers throughout this very County of Londonderry. Now, this suggestion must have probably originated with the Londoners themselves, whose agents, although not permitted to lodge in these houses, had learned to covet them. Then these worthy citizens were not, on any pretext, to be permitted to listen to any stories tending to inspire them with a "fear of the Irish"—and this was well ordered—for the London Companies afterwards found these Irish to be their best friends, and rather than part with their services were willing to incur the displeasure, and even the threatened hostility, of the Government. It so happened that the London Companies could get very few British tenant-settlers to risk themselves either in O'Cahan's country or in Loughinsholin, where the people kept so many pikes, and perhaps the only one advantage of having them (the Companies) in Ulster at all was, that these Companies, although for their own interests, were a principal means of preserving the Irish race from utter extinction in our Northern province. At all events, the Companies stoutly maintained the right of holding the Irish as their tenants, of preventing their expulsion; and to these Londoners we are indebted, more perhaps than to the servitors or Bishops, for the thriving and vigorous native population in Ulster at the present day. Indeed, this whole business furnishes a curious illustration of the following words of the poet :—

The best laid schemes of mice and men
Gang aft aglee,
And leave them nought but grief and pain
For promised joy.

In the meantime, whilst the Commissioners at Limavady were beginning to fear that they had been labouring there in vain, the four London citizens arrived at the camp—even as the official party were collecting their traps to depart. Davys immediately informed Salisbury of their arrival, on the 28th of August, 1609, in the following terms :—" The Londoners are now come and are exceeding welcome. We all use our best rhetoric to persuade them to go on with their plantation, which will assure this whole island to the Crown of England for ever. They like and praise the country very much, specially the Banne and the river of Loughfeyle. One of the agents is fallen sick, and would fain return ; but the Lord Deputy and all the rest here use means to comfort him, and to retain him, lest this accident should discourage his fellow-citizens." We have a much more interesting account of the Londoners' four agents in a letter written by Chichester from the " Camp in Fermanagh, near Ennishkeelyn, 18 September, 1609." " Sir Thomas Phillips," he writes, " with the four agents of London, came into me likewise in the County of Coleraine. They landed at Knockfergus, and in their way from thence they beheld Coleraine and the River Banne beneath the Leape ; they have now seen the Derry, the river of Loughfoyle, the Lyffer [Lifford], and sundry parts adjoining, and they like so well of the sates, the lands adjoining the rivers, and the commodities they think to raise by their purse and good husbandry, that they assure me the city of London will really undertake the plantation upon the report they are to make, and that with expedition. If they should not, as I have often told them, they will be enemies to themselves, for the fishings, lands, and woods, with toleration of custom and other privileges, which his Majesty has graciously proffered to them, are worth not less than £2,000 a year as they now are, and their purse and industry will, within two or three years, improve them to double that value. They came in a convenient time, when the people in each county made their appearance, declaring their obedience and submission to the law in a far better fashion than within these three years I ever expected to have seen within this province; and if my good usage, and that of the Council with me, could add to the other encouragements they have found, it has not been and shall not be wanting. I advised them to send an assay of the commodities which the country at this time afforded to the Lord Mayor, of which they took good liking; and so I procured them raw hides, tallow, salmon, herrings, eels, pipe staves, beef, and the like, at easy prices. I also procured them some of the iron ore, and will add specimens of the lead and copper. They are now gone to take a more exact view of the River Banne above the Leape, and of the woods of Glankonkyne and Kylletra, intending to meet me about fourteen days hence, upon my return towards Dublin. Sir Thomas Phillips, to his charge and trouble, daily accompanies them from one place to another, which is a great comfort to them. He will return with them; and in the meantime nothing shall be wanting to continue them in the resolution they have taken; for albeit I perceive they aim at some things that yield no profit, yet I will not hinder so good a work—the best that ever was undertaken in my time for the general good of the kingdom—for my own private ends, as I doubt not they will declare unto your Lordship."

From this point the negotiations between the Council in London and the Corporation went forward without a hitch until the whole arrangements were completed. The deputies on their return from Ulster gave a glowing but strictly true account of "O'Cahan's fertile country"—which they represented as "fertile" in every respect—in its soil so well suited to the rearing of all sorts of cattle, and the cultivation of every useful crop—in its rivers and coasts, so abundant in the production of fish and fowl—in its woods, which were then the haunts of the red deer, and in which the Englishmen were astounded by the size and magnificence of the forest trees, especially the oaks and elms—in its mineral wealth, where the "smiths made iron before their faces, and of the iron they made steel within less than one hour," from the ore which could be gathered in some districts even from the surface—in its springs and brooks, which everywhere delighted the eyes of the strangers—and even in its bogs, which they reported as affording "plenty of good and wholesome turf to supply the want of other fuel." When this report was read, and when, in addition, the Aldermen saw the magnificent samples of eels, fresh herrings, salmon, beef, and tallow which Chichester had wisely got under their very eyes, there was no longer any doubt about the destiny of "O'Cahan's fertile country;" it was thenceforth to be taken into the possession of twelve London Companies, with a Society to act as an intermediate link between these Companies and the Crown, and which Society is generally known as the Irish Society, but by its own special baptism is styled "The Honourable Society of the Governor and Assistants, London, of the New Plantation in Ulster, within the Realm of Ireland." The twelve Companies were Goldsmiths, Grocers, Fishmongers, Ironmongers, Mercers, Merchant-Tailors, Haberdashers, Clothworkers, Skinners, Vintners, Drapers, and Salters.

When these Companies or Associations had been twelve months in possession of their several estates in Londonderry, Sir George

Carew reported very briefly and unfavourably of them as follows:—"In the County of Colrane we neither found nor understood of anything done by the Londoners towards the performance of the Articles of the Plantation. Their agents receive the rents there, and in the barony of Lough-Enish O'Lyn, from the natives, and seek not to remove them, which makes the said natives to conceive that they shall not be displanted; which is a great hindrance to the plantation of that county, and ill example to their neighbours. The first buildings of which we took note were at Colrane, where we saw a good rampier of earth and sods raised 6 foot high and 12 or 14 foot thick, round about the town, and the bulwarks of same height, the ditch digged about 3 feet deep, and near the full breadth of 36 or 40 foot; a mill-dam with a bank at the head of the pond of 300 foot long and 40 foot broad, and 14 or 15 foot deep, with two very fair flood-gates lined with strong oaken timber and planks; a fair mill-house, 25 foot long and 22 in breadth, of one storie high—three mills in the same house, one for wheat, one for malt, and the third a truck mill; a very fair pound of sawn oak timber, 40 foot square; a bridge or wharf made in the Bann, of 60 foot long and 12 broad, of very strong oak timber, clasped together in the joints with bars and bolts of iron. Sir Thomas Phillips, Knight, hath erected a water-mill at Limavadie, unto which he drew water a mile, in a sluice or pond 12 foot broad and 5 foot deep; he hath put in good forwardness an inn builded English fashion, for the relief of passengers passing that way. He hath, towards the building the new Castle of Lemavadie, felled and squared in the woods of Glenconkeyne good store of timber, and hath raised stone out of the ditch adjoining the old Castle, being a very hard rock, whereby he intends to make some good work for the defence of the country. Captain Edward Doddington hath builded at Dungiven a Castle of

22 foot broad and four stories high, whereof some part of the walls were standing before, and is now by him well finished and slated; he hath built a house adjoining to the Castle 43 foot long and 18 broad, the walls whereof some parts were standing, but now very well and handsomely slated and finished; he hath repaired a bawne of lime and stone about the castle and house. We next came to Derry, where we saw the church well slated and repaired; two fair houses of stone, two stories high, slated and finished, with cellars; a thatched house wherein Mr. Wray dwelleth; a sawpit covered with deal boards; a smith's forge, with a dwell-house to the same; two lime-kilns; a wharf 300 foot long and 14 broad; a bark building, of 70 or 80 tons, with provisions of plank and other timber for her. The Fort of Deserte Martyne, a place in Glenconkeyne, is thought fit for the King's service, and the service of travellers between Coleraine and all parts of Tyrone and Armagh, to be laid out with 300 acres for a fort. The London agents have agreed to the place and number of acres, but in regard that Deserte Martyne, on which the forte is to be erected, is the Bishop of Derry's land. We think fit that the Londoners should give him so much in exchange thereof of their own land, and we think it not amiss that the King should give £200 towards erecting the fort, the constable to pay the overplus, if any."

IV

THE Company of Goldsmiths was the first of those mentioned on the foregoing list. This Company's lands are situated in the barony of Tirkeerin, and border on the County Tyrone northward, their other boundaries being chiefly the Lough and River of Foyle. Pynnar states that the agent of this Company in 1620 was

John Freeman, Esq. The Goldsmiths were the first amongst several other companies to dispose of their lands in perpetuity, reserving small rents generally between £400 and £500. So early as the year 1730 the Goldsmiths sold their manor, known as Goldsmiths' Hall, to the Earl of Shelburne, for the sum of £14,100, and a reserved rent of £450. This small head-rent gives the Goldsmiths still a semblance of authority on their lands, and the Irish Society is thus privileged to go through a formal routine of suggestions as to the management of the estate. In 1838, these lands, which had long previously passed from the Shelburne family, are referred to in the Society's Report for that year, as follows:—"This estate has been miserably neglected, but we hope, now that the whole is in possession of Leslie Alexander, Esq., of Foyle Park, he will immediately attend to the performance of those duties incumbent on him as the possessor of this proportion." The Society's advice will have since, no doubt, been addressed to several other holders of fragments of the Goldsmiths' lands, for the family of Alexander, in 1875, retained not much over 5,000 acres of the same. These fragments now comprise many thousands of acres, although the Goldsmiths' grant only originally conveyed to that Company 3,210 acres.

2. The Grocers' lands lie also in the barony of Tirkeerin. The manor of Muff, or Grocers' Hall, is bounded on the north by Lough Foyle, and extends southward as far as the Burntollet River; its western boundary is the River Foyle, and eastward it meets the lands of an adjoining proportion. When Pynnar came—1618-1620—he found the Grocers' agent, Edward Rowan, Esq., just dead, and the whole estate neglected, and lying in confusion. There were some buildings, but chiefly done by a few tenants, although they got no tenures, and informed Pynnar that they were likely to be removed, although some of them had severally

expended £100 in improvements. All the lands, with slight exceptions, were occupied by the Irish, the former owners. Seven of the companies, the Grocers included, leased their lands to persons who had come as their agents, and generally for terms of 61 years and three lives. Some considerable time after Rowan's death, a Mr. Babington became the Grocers' tenant, and devoted himself very efficiently to the task of making up for previous neglect. It may, therefore, be supposed that the Irish Society would be pleased at last with the state of affairs on the Grocers' lands. After having made many unfavourable reports, the Society was able to affirm in 1838 that the "Grocers' proportion, next to the Drapers', is the best managed estate." The chief town is Muff, which is a very neat and clean place, with an excellent church and market-house and other buildings. It appears from a comparatively recent return of owners of land in Ireland that the Grocers' Company hold 11,638 acres, nearly four times the quantity conveyed in their grant.

3. The Fishmongers' lands lie partly in the barony of Keenaght and partly in that of Tirkeerin. The lands in Keenaght lie along the eastern and southern shores of Lough Foyle, and those in Tirkeerin extend from Faughanvale in the north to a place called Feeny in the south. In Pynnar's time the Fishmongers had let this property to a London merchant named Higgins, whose agent dwelt at Fishmongers' Hall, *alias* Ballykellie, and near this place, Pynnar reports, there was then "a good preacher to teach the people." In Samson's "Memoir of Chart," and when referring to good residences in this district, he mentions that a "Mr. Sterling had a good dwelling on the site of the ancient castle of the Fishmongers' proportion. Here also are the earliest gardens in the county, well enclosed with walls and stored with excellent fruit trees." The Fishmongers hold 20,509 acres, or nearly seven

times the quantity conveyed in their grant from the Crown.

4. The Ironmongers' proportion, known as the manor of Lizard, is situated in the barony of Coleraine, between the Bann on the east and the barony of Keenaght on the west. Pynnar reported that "George Cammynge (Canning), agent for the Company, is here resident; but he hath no order to make any estates to any tenants that are come hither to dwell, notwithstanding there are divers that have disbursed a great deal of money and built houses. Besides, here is an infinite number of Irish upon the land, which give such great rents that the English cannot get any land." The Irish cheerfully submitted to rack-renting rather than being disturbed in their old cherished houses. The lands of this manor extend more or less into the five parishes of Aghadowey, Agivey, Desertoghill, Errigal, and Macosquin. The Ironmongers leased their lands in 1705, 1725, 1766, and 1813 respectively to George Canning, jun., Henry Lecky, Josias Du Pré, and Sir William C. Beresford. The Company holds at the present time 12,714 acres, or four times the quantity conveyed in their grant from the Crown.

5. The Mercers' lands lie in part along the Bann, in the barony of Coleraine, but by much the larger portion is situated in the barony of Loughinsholin, extending southward from the Ironmongers' proportion as far as a little stream called Ennivaroy, and a locality known as Granahan. The ruins of the castle called Mercers' Hall still exist in the townland of Movanagher, parish of Kilrea. In 1620 Pynnar reported that the Mercers' lands were not "set to any man as yet, but held by one Vernon, agent for the Company. Not far from the Bawne there are six houses of cage-work, inhabited by such poor men as they could find in the country, and these pay such dear rates for the land that they are forced to take Irish tenants under them to pay

the rent. There are divers other houses of slight building, but they are far off, and dwell dispersedly in the woods, where they are forced of mere necessity to relieve such woodkearn as go up and down the country; and, as I am informed by diverse in the country, there are forty-six townlands of this proportion that are set to the Irish of the sept of Clandonnells (descendants of a Donald O'Neill), which are the wickedest men in all the country." The Mercers now hold 21,241 acres, or over seven times as much as was conveyed to them in their grant from the Crown.

6. The Merchant Tailors' proportion is situated in the northern half of the barony of Coleraine. Along the Bann, its eastern boundary, it reaches from near Killowen, in a southern direction, as far as a place called Curragh, the intermediate localities along this eastern border being Somerset, Ballynas, Castleroe, Camus, Coole, and Ballylaggan. Westward the lands of this proportion extend as far as the boundary line between the baronies of Coleraine and Keenaght. Pynnar reported in 1620 that the manor of "Merchant Tailors' Hall, *alias* Macosquin, is in the hands of Valentine Hartopp, Esq., who is newly come to dwell there, having taken this proportion of the Company for 61 years." This Company is one of four who granted their lands in perpetuity for small yearly head rents and large fines or purchase money. In this case the purchaser was a Mr. Richardson, whose present representative holds 18,159, although this quantity does not include all the lands belonging to the estate. The whole lands are more than seven times as much as was originally granted to the Tailors from the Crown.

7. The Haberdashers' lands lie along the eastern boundary in the barony of Keenaght, commencing on the skirts of Benevenagh in the north, and reaching southward as far as Formil and Camnish, on the eastern and western slopes of the Benbradach

mountain range. Pynnar reported that the manor of "Haberdashers' Hall, *alias* Ballycastle, was taken by Sir Robert M'Lellan for 61 years, and upon this proportion the castle is strongly finished, being very strong and well wrought, himself with his lady and family dwelling in it." Sir Robert MacLellan was son in-law to Sir Hugh Montgomery, first Lord Ards, but neither he ner his lady lived long after Pynnar's visit in 1618-20. The Haberdashers sold their lands in perpetuity to the Beresfords, whose residence therein was known as Walworth. The Marquis of Waterford, the representative of Beresford, sold recently to Sir H. H. Bruce 20,801 acres of the Haberdashers' lands; whilst John B. Beresford, Esq., still holds 10,420 acres of the same property, so that this estate is more than ten times as large as the quantity conveyed in that grant from the Crown.

8. The Clothworkers' proportion occupies the most northern position in the barony of Coleraine, extending from the shore of the Atlantic, in a south-western direction, as far as Killowen, and along its western border as far southward as Formoyle. Pynnar reports that Sir Robert MacLellan had rented this proportion also, and that it was entirely inhabited by Irish, the only British freeholder being the parson of the parish. The Clothworkers sold their lands in perpetuity to the Bruce family for a large sum, reserving a small head rent. The most notable place of residence on these lands is Downhill, whose picturesque beauty has been duly noticed by the Rev. G. V. Samson thus:—"Amidst these rude masses winding walks are laid out with taste; the nakedness is generally relieved by abundant crops of grasses, and not unfrequently the brow of a rude ledge is decorated by the rich yellow and green of various trefoils, sea pinks, and sea-campions."

9. The Skinners' lands lie in the three baronies of Loughinsholin, Keenaght, and Tirkeerin.

Pynnar reported that the manor of "Skinners' Hall, *alias* Dungevan, was in the possession of Lady Dodington, wife of the late Sir Edward Dodington, she having taken a grant of it from the Company for 61 years." This Lady Dodington, who was a daughter of Tristram Beresford, the Irish Society's first agent, was residing in Skinners' Hall, at Dungiven, "with 24 in her family," during Pynnar's visit. She soon afterwards remarried with Sir Francis Cooke. The Skinners have frequently let their lands by lump to great advantage, getting so much as £25,000 at one haul, on a terminable lease, from a Mr. Ogilvie, a Dublin linen manufacturer. The Irish Society report in 1838 that they are "Sorry to say that this property is proverbial throughout the County of Derry for that lack of comfort among the tenantry so much deplored in some parts of Ireland." The Company is now in exclusive possession of 34,772 acres, or between eleven and twelve times as much land as was conveyed to it in the grant from the Crown.

10. The Vintners' lands, known as Bellaghy, from the principal town therein, are situated in the barony of Loughinsholin, and extend from the Mercers' proportion, in a southern direction near the Bann, as far as the shore of Lough Beg, and westward at one point to the boundary between this barony and Keenaght. Pynnar reported that the manor of Vintners' Hall was in the hands of Baptist Jones, Esq., who was then resident, with his wife and family. The Vintners' Company was one of the four who sold their lands in perpetuity, reserving a small head rent. This sale was made in 1736, the purchaser, Mr. Conolly, of Castletown, paying the Vintners £15,000—a goodly sum at that period. Mr. Samson refers to this district as follows :—"There is a good number of trees scattered about Mrs. Downing's house at Rose-Gift, and at the old castle of Bellaghy some fine old timber. Mr. Spottiswood has planted with good success at

Bellaghy. Near to Portglenone Mr. Ellis, of Innisrush, and Mr. Courtney, of Glenowen, have respectable residences and plantations."

11. The Drapers' lands, also in the barony of Loughinsholin, extend southward as far as the County of Tyrone, and westward to Glenshane and the vicinity of Desertmartin. Pynnar reported that at the time of his visit Drapers' Hall, *alias* Moneymore, was "not set to any man, but held by the agent, Mr. Russell." Much of this proportion adjoins the mountain of Slievegallon. Great improvements were made in this district from the time the Drapers secured the services of a Mr. Rowley Miller as agent. In 1838 the report of the Irish Society speaks in rapturous terms of these improvements. "We were very much pleased," say the deputies, "in going through this proportion. The chief town, Moneymore, is quite an English town, most beautifully laid out and managed by Mr. Rowley Miller and his son. The inn is one of the best we met whilst in Ireland. The Company have lately established another town called Drapers' Town, which is thriving rapidly. There are many thriving plantations of timber here; and the whole appearances of the farm-houses, and the town, with the church, the market-house, and other buildings, all indicate the kindness of the Drapers' Company, and of their excellent manager, Mr. Miller." The Drapers hold 27,025 acres, or about nine times the quantity of land conveyed in their grant from the Crown.

12. The Salters' lands lie also in the barony of Loughinsholin, and extend from the Vintners' proportion along the shore of Lough Neagh to Ballinderry, on the confines of Tyrone. The Salters' agent in Pynnar's time was a Mr. Hugh Sayers, and the Company had commenced to build Magherafelt and Salters' Town. The Salters' lands were leased for years only, when Samson wrote his "Memoir" in 1814, and probably for long periods before and after

that date. He states that it was the only manor or proportion of the twelve so managed. The Salters changed this system of letting their lands before the year 1838, as at that date they had demised the whole manor for a term of years, receiving a large fine from the lessee. The Irish Society's report in 1838 states that "the Salters' estate is one of the four proportions which is leased for a term of years; in other words, it is for a time out of their hands, and consequently out of the management of the Company. The lease granted by the Company will expire in 1853. This proportion, however, is most fortunate in having such a landlord as Sir Robert Bateson, the member for the county, who holds directly from the Company." The Salters now hold 19,445 acres, or between six and seven times as much as was conveyed to them by their original grant from the Crown.

These Londoners have had a stormy career in Ulster, but as that career is probably soon to terminate, it is not necessary here to particularise the number and variety of their triumphs. They have swept enormous wealth from this "howling wilderness" between the Foyle and the Bann since 1610; and they must have had pretty jolly times in their intervals from anxiety and labour, as it is admitted that they have spent £75,000 a year on dinners. Who would not be civilisers and suppressors of Irish barbarism?

THE COUNTY OF DONEGAL.

I.

Until the commencement of the seventeenth century this vast region was known as Tyrconnell, and in very early Irish history as Cinel-Conaill, or the country of the descendants of Conall Gulban. These descendants were the celebrated Clann-Dalaigh, of "Brown Shields," so named from Dalach, one of their most distinguished chiefs, who died in the year 868. From his grandson Domhnall (pronounced Donnell) this great race or tribe derived its hereditary surname of O'Donnell. The O'Neills and O'Donnells were kindred races, both being descended from a common ancestor, and this relationship was not unfrequently and not unnaturally, appealed to as a reason for political union on any great emergency. This appeal was uniformly successful until the time of the English invasion; but, very soon afterwards, the O'Donnells began to transfer their allegiance occasionally to the Saxons, as by so doing they found that they could better extend their own territory in the North-West of Ulster. Between the years 640 and 1207, the O'Donnells were lords only of one cantred, of which Kilmacrenan was the most noted district, but subsequently, by the aid of English soldiers, they became princes of all Tirconnell. This position was retained by their chiefs until the close of the sixteenth century, when the Northern lords lost everything in the course of the seven years' war against the Government. Tyrconnell lost even its ancient and proud name; and it was only left for Tyrconnell's last hereditary Bard to contrast mournfully the loneliness of his chieftain's grave in a foreign land with the deeply sympathetic honours and regrets which would have distinguished it had he died in his native Ulster. Hear how he apostrophises Nuala O'Donnell as she weeps by her brother's grave :—

O woman of the piercing wail,
  Who mournest o'er yon mound of clay
    With sigh and groan !
Would God thou wert among the Gael !
  Thou would'st not then from day to day
    Weep thus alone.
'Twere long before, around a grave
  In green Tyrconnell, one could find
    This loneliness.
Near where Beann Boirche's banners wave
  Such grief as thine could ne'er have pined
    Companionless.

Beside the wave in Donegal,
  In Antrim's glens, or fair Dromore,
    Or Killilea ;
Or where the sunny waters fall
  At Assaroe, near Erna's shore,
    This could not be !
On Derry's plains, in rich Drumcleiff,
  Throughout Armagh the great, renowned
    In older years—
No day could pass but woman's grief
  Would rain upon this burial ground
    Fresh floods of tears.

Oh no ! from Shannon, Boyne, and Suir,
  From high Dunluce's castle walls,
    From Lissnadill,
Would flock alike both rich and poor,
  One wail would rise from Cruachan's halls,
    To Tara's hill !
And some would come from Barrow's side,
  And many a maid would leave her home
    On Leitrim's plains,
And by melodious Banna's tide,
  And by the Mourne and Erne, to come
    And swell thy strains.

The "country" of the O'Donnells, now Donegal, contains no less than 1,193,443 acres. When Dr. Beaufort drew up his admirable "Memoir of a Map of Ireland," there were forty-two parishes in this county, containing on an average 16,179 acres each, thirty of these parishes being in the diocese of Raphoe, eleven in that of Derry, and only one in the bishoprick of Clogher. According to the census of 1831 the number of parishes has been considerably increased since Beaufort published his "Memoir," the barony of Inishowen now containing twelve parishes and two extra-parochial districts; Raphoe, eleven whole parishes and parts of two other parishes; Tyrhugh, four whole parishes and part of four other parishes; Bannagh, seven whole parishes, and part of another parish; Boylagh, three whole parishes, and part of another parish; and Kilmacrenan, twelve whole parishes, and part of another parish. The present County of Donegal contains six baronies, namely, Inishowen in the north, Raphoe in the east, Tyrhugh and Boylagh in the west, Bannagh in the south-west, and Kilmacrenan in the north-west.

The Plantation Commissioners did not include the great barony of Inishowen in their operations, as it had been handed over by the Crown to Chichester by way of a reward for his effective services in smoothing up the various rough and noisy places throughout Ulster. They found that in Donegal there were certain native chiefs of small septs who had owned lands independently of O'Donnel, and whose claims the Commissioners were disposed to allow, but eventually these claimants had to rest and content themselves with comparatively small portions as undertakers, although they had taken the part of the Government in the preceding struggle. They were fortunate, however, in obtaining any terms, for Chichester disliked every mother's son of them, and had in his "Notes of Remembrances" prejudiced the London authorities against them. "Divers gentlemen," said he, "claim freeholds in that country, as, namely, the three septs of the M'Swynes, Banagh, Fanaght, and Doe; also O'Boyle and O'Gallagher; but these men passed over their rights, if any they had, to the Earl [Rorie O'Donnell], which he got from them cautiously, and by unworthy means; and I am sure all of them have more land than they or their septs will be able to manure and plant in any civil fashion these forty years, albeit peace did continue among them; and they are for the most part unworthy of what they possess, being a people inclined to blood and trouble, but to displant them is very difficult. If his Majesty disposes of the land to strangers, they [the strangers] must be very powerful to suppress them. I suggest that if his pleasure be to continue them in what they claim, the lands may be divided into many parts, and disposed to several men of the septs, and some to strangers or others of this nation, leaving none greater than another, unless it be in a small difference to the now chiefs of the name."

The Commissioners divided the whole county, exclusive of Inishowen, into six great plantation precincts—namely, Portlough, Liffer, Doe, Faynaght, Boylagh, and Banagh, and Tyrhugh. They commenced with the Liffer or Lifford, in which they found 15,000 arable acres, marking this quantity off into eleven proportions, which were afterwards allotted, with some slight exceptions, to nine English undertakers. This precinct of the Liffer formed the greater part of the present barony of Raphoe, which contains 220,723 acres, containing part of the parishes of Cornwall and Arney, with the whole of the parishes of All Saints, Clonleigh, Convoy, Donaghmore, Killea, Kiltevogue, Leck, Raphoe, Raymoghy, Stranorlar, and Toughboyne; its towns and principal villages being Newtowncunningham, Ballindrait, Convoy, Castlefinn, Carrigans, Raphoe, Manorcunningham, Ballybofey, Killygordon, Stranorlar, Creaghdoss, St. Johnston, and part of Lifford. The names of the English planters to whom this great sweep of territory was allotted were Henry Clare of Stanfield Hall, in the County of Norfolk, Esq.; Edward Russell, Esq.; Sir William Barnes, Knight; Captain Ralph Mansfield; Sir Thomas Cornewall, Knight;

Sir Thomas Remyngton, Knight; Sir Maurice Berkeley, Knight; and Sir Thomas Coach, Knight. These planters had, it will be admitted, vast scopes on which to augment their several estates, when it is considered that all the waste or unprofitable lands were thrown in gratuitously to the several proportions.

After they had been twelve months in occupation, Sir George Carew made the following report from this precinct of the Liffer, or Raphoe:—"Sir Henry Dowra, Knight, undertaker of 2,000 acres, has by allowance of the Council passed over his portion of land to William Wilson, of Clayre, in Suffolk, who has letters patent in his own name. The said Wilson had his agent, Chris. Parmenter, resident, who appeared before us. There are some families of English resident, who brought over good store of household stuff, and have stock 21 cows and oxen, nine mares, one service horse, and some small cattle. Sir Morris Barkley, Knight, undertaker of 2,000 acres; has not been here, nor any agent for him; nothing done. Sir Robert Remyngton, Knight, 2,000 acres; the like [*i.e.* nothing done]. Sir Thomas Cornewall, Knight; 2,000 acres; his agent, Edward Littleton, took possession, and is resident; has built nothing, nor provided any materials yet. Sir William Barnes, Knight; 1,500 acres; sold his proportion to Edward Russell, who is possessed, but has done nothing. Sir Henry Clare, Knight; 1,500 acres; has an agent resident named William Browne; nothing done. Sir Thomas Coach, Knight; 1,500 acres; is resident; has built a large timber house, adjoining to the castle of Skarfollis, and is providing materials for re-edifying the castle; four families of British upon his lands, to whom he intends to pass estates. Captain Edward Russell, 1,500 acres; is resident, and his son with him; there are two English houses of timber framed; stock, four horses, six English cows, and a bull; three or four English labourers, but no tenants. Captain Mansfield, 1,000 acres; is resident, but has done nothing. Town of Lyffer, a good and strong fort of lime and stone, built by Sir Richard Hansard, towards which the King allowed him £200 English. Sir Richard Hansard, being appointed by the now Lord Deputy to be at Lyffer [Lifford] with his company in 1607, found but one house in that town. Upon view of the town we found it [1611] well furnished with inhabitants of English, and Scottish, and Irish, who live by several trades, brought thither by Sir Richard, who built twenty-one houses for tenants who are to give entertainment to passengers. Thirty seven houses are built by others. Town of Donegall; we found a fair bawne built, with flankers, and a parapet, and a walk on the top, fifteen foot high. Within the bawne is a strong house of stone, built by Captain Basill Brooke, towards which the King gave him £250 English. Many families of English, Scottish, and Irish are inhabiting in the town, who built them good copled houses after the manner of the Pale. About two miles from thence Captain Paul Gore has erected a fair stone house out of the ruins of O'Boyle's old castle upon the seaside, which he has by direction af the Lords of the Council delivered up to Laird Broughton, undertaker of those lands; he demands some consideration for his charges, which we think him worthy of."

When the Commissioners saw the old monastery at Donegal—which had been founded by the beautiful Nuala O'Donnell, *alias* O'Connor, in 1474, and in which the Four Masters had compiled their "Annals of Ireland—the first idea that occurred to them [the Commissioners] was that it should be allotted to the Bishop of Raphoe for his habitation, "reserving sufficient room for the school and schoolmaster." A friar who had sojourned in this religious house several years described its position and surroundings in the following terms:—"The site, indeed, was happily chosen, and nothing could surpass the beauty of the prospect which it commanded. Hard by the windows of the refectory was the wharf, where foreign ships took in their cargoes of hides, fish, wool, and linen cloth; and there, too, came the galleons of Spain, laden with wine and arms, in exchange for the merchandise which the Lords of Tyrconnell sent annually to the Brabant marts, then the great emporium for the North of Europe. In sooth, it was a lovely spot, and sweetly suggestive of holy meditations. In the calm days of summer, when the broad expanse of the estuary lay still and unruffled, mirroring in its blue depths the over-canopying heaven, was it not a fair image of the unbroken tranquillity and peace to which the hearts of the recluses aspired? And in the gloomy winter nights, when the great crested waves rolled in majestic fury against the granite headlands, would not the driving storm and unavailing cry of drowning mariners remind the inmate of that monastery that he had chosen the safer part, by abandoning a world where the tempest of the passions wreaks destruction far more appalling." Leaving the poor friar's argument for a monastic life at what it is worth, it is gratifying to know that this venerable old pile was left by the planting prowlers to crumble away in peace. It would have been such a startling contrast to have had it occupied by a worldly though clever prelate, as George Montgomery was! And think, too, that in the library of this ruin was found the famous *Liber Hymnorum*, which is believed to be over a thousand years old, and which is, indeed, such a noble monument of the attainments of an Irish monk. More than eleven centuries ago, in the little island of Iniscaltra, on Lough Derg, the monk Camin was able to collate the Vulgate with the Hebrew text, and to enrich his copy of the work "with a lucid interpretation of obscure words and passages." The facts, too, that Nuala O'Donnell died before the completion of her religious house, and was buried in a vault under the grand altar, are of themselves enough to secure for its remaining fragment the veneration of all who are cognisant of them. But how few of those who have had to deal with Ulster as governors know anything of its history! In 1566, Sir Henry Sydney, during one of his excursions to the North, visited the monastery of Donegal, looked at it, and left it with this reflection:—"We left behind us a house of Observant Friars, unspoiled or hurt, and with small cost fortifiable, much accommodated with the nearness of the water, and with fair groves, orchards, and gardens, which are about the same." He and others of his class only contemplated how such places could be best utilised as defences against the people who had built them, and had cherished them as places of worship.

II.

It would appear from Carew's report that these English planters who had been allotted such broad lands in the Liffer were not in haste to commence their "civilising" operations there. 1. Henry Clare, who came from the County of Norfolk, did not long retain his Ulster lands, and, although he was knighted about the time he got out his patent, he could not be drawn, even for a short visit, from Stanfield Hall. He sold his proportion of Shragmirlar to Peter Benson, who let or leased the lands thereon to the following-named British settlers, viz.:—Sir Ralph Bingley, Robert Kilpatterick, James Kilpatterick, Archibald M'Math, James Maxwell, James Tate, John Ewart, Thomas Watson, George Newton, Ludovic Stubbins, George Hilton, George Baillie, Richard Roper, James Reid, Henry Atkinson, Sir Richard Hansard, Richard Babington, Edward Catherall, and John Kilpatterick. 2. William Wilson came from Bolton, in the County of Suffolk, and appears to have been a persevering planter. The date of his death is not mentioned in any printed inquisition, but in 1635 his son, Sir John Wilson, was in possession not only of the originally granted proportion of Aghagalla, but of another, called Convoigh, together with additional parcels in the same district, all of which were created the manor of Wilsonsfort. In 1629 Sir John Wilson, who was known as of Killenure, County Donegal, was nominated by Sir Frederick Hamilton to be raised to the dignity of a baronet, pursuant to the authority given by a King's letter. Sir Frederick Hamilton was the youngest brother of the Earl of Abercorn, and had got from the King authority to nominate two baronets, for the proper negotiating of which both he and the King were well paid by the persons receiving the title. In 1629 also, a grant was made to Sir John Wilson, Knight and Baronet, of the two proportions above named, and other lands, amounting to 926 acres, all in the precinct of Liffer and barony of Raphoe. Sir John died in 1636, and his only child Anne, then two years of age, died in 1639. The property was then inherited by Andrew Wilson, a brother of Sir John. 3. Edward Russell came from London, and was styled "Captain" by Pynnar. He soon sold his proportion, called Acharine, to Sir John Kingsmill, who resold a portion of the lands to William Wilson above-mentioned. Kingsmill had a grant in 1630 of more than 2,000 acres adjoining Castlefinn. The old Irish castle there was repaired and used by Sir John Kingsmill as his stated place of residence. There had been a dispute about the possession of this building between Russell, the first patentee, and Bishop George Montgomery. The latter claimed it as standing on Church land, but failed to establish his claim. 4. Sir William Barnes must have been introduced by some potent friend, probably the King, as an undertaker. He was knighted in 1611, and sold his proportion called Marrister to Captain Edward Russell above named. The latter resold in turn to Sir John Kingsmill and William Wilson, and eventually both the proportions of Acharine and Marrister were included in the Wilsonfort estate. 5. Ralph Mansfield's former place of residence in England is not known. He dwelt on his proportion of Kilnorguerdan, now Killygordon, near Stranorlar, until the time of his death in 1634. He had disputes with two neighbouring planters, viz., Sir John Davy's and Captain Russell—about mearings, which disputes were eventually settled favourably for him. He was succeeded by his son, John Mansfield, who was of age at the time of his father's death, and married. The estate of Killygordon lies in the vale of the Finn, between Stranorlar and Strabane. Francis Mansfield, Esq., of Ardrummon House, is the present (1878) representative of the original patentee, and is in possession of the actual patent from James I. to Captain Ralph Mansfield. He is descended maternally from the Montgomery family of Eglinton, in Ayrshire. 6. Sir Thomas Cornwall was son and heir of Thomas Cornwall, Baron of Burford, in Salop, and Gentleman of the Privy Chamber to the King's son, Prince Henry. In 1610 Sir Thomas wrote to Salisbury from Burford, in Herefordshire, requesting to be left out of the sheriff's roll for that county, because of his necessary attendance on the Prince of Wales, and also because of his having no present residence in Herefordshire. He quickly disposed of his proportion of Corlackin to Robert Davies, and the latter let it out to Irish tenants of a respectable standing. 7. Sir Thomas Remyngton was vice-president of Munster, and appears to have soon sold his proportion of Tawnaforis to Sir Ralph Bingley. The latter soon afterwards died, and in 1628 there was a Crown grant of Tawnaforis, 2,000 acres, and Lurga, 1,000 acres, to Lady Anne Binglie. Her Ladyship's trustees were John, Earl of Bridgewater, William Ravenscroft, Edward Orwell, and Henry Skipwith, Esqrs. This grant conveyed the advowson of the rectory of Donaghmore and a free fishing in the water of Lough Swilly. Soon after the date of the above-mentioned grant, Lady Bingley married Robert Harrington, Esq., and in May, 1630, the lands of Tawnaforis were granted to her second husband and herself, or the longer liver of them—the proportion of Tawnaforis to be called the manor of Orwell. 8. Sir Maurice Berkely was the leader of a small company of undertakers seeking for lands either in Oneilan or the Liffer. He came from Somersetshire, and wanted to undertake 4,000 acres, but he was eventually satisfied with half the quantity—or the two proportions of Dromore and Lurga, each containing 1,000 acres. Sir Maurice married Elizabeth, daughter of Sir William Killegrew, of Hanworth. He was father of the Sir John Berkeley, so much distinguished for his services in the reign of Charles I., and for which he was created in 1658 Baron Berkeley, of Stratton. Berkeley sold his two proportions to Sir Ralph Bingley, and these lands in 1630 were granted to Lady Bingley and her second husband, Robert Harrington, Esq. Dromore and Lurga were created a manor, known as the manor of Burleigh. 9. Sir Thomas Coach (whose surname has been written also Coath, Cootch, and Coates), was a good servitor in the South of Ireland, where his services pleased Chichester so well that the latter wrote from London requesting that Coach, "who served well in the wars of Ireland, be remembered for some parcel of land in the Northern plantation." He obtained the middle proportion of 1,500 acres, called Frikeanagh, but afterwards known to Pynnar as Lismonagan. On this proportion stood the castle of Skarfollie, the site of which also was claimed by Bishop Montgomery as Church lands, but his claim was not allowed. Sir Thomas Coach died in May, 1620, and was succeeded by his son Henry, then twelve years of age.

The next plantation precinct in Donegal which claimed the attention of the Commissioners was that which they named, for convenience, Portlough—a name which has long since become obsolete. The precinct, however, comprised a section of the barony of Raphoe, together with a section of the territory now known as the baronies of Boylagh and Bannagh. In Portlough the Commissioners found 12,000 arable acres, which quantity was marked off into twelve proportions of 1,000 acres each, and afterwards distributed amongst nine Scottish undertakers. The names of these planters were—the Duke of Lennox, Sir Walter Stewart, laird of Minto; Alexander M'Aula, of Durlin, gent.; John Cuningham, of Crawfield, gent.; William Stewart, laird of Dunduff; James Cunyngham, laird of Glengarnock; Cuthbert Cuningham, gent.; James Cuningham, Esq., and John Stewart, Esq. Of these Scottish undertakers Sir George Carew reported, after they had twelve months' occupancy of their several proportions, as follows:—"Duke of Lennox, chief undertaker of 2,000 acres; Sir Aulant Aula, Knight, his agent resident, with some British families; no preparation for building save some timber trees felled and squared. Sir Walter Stewart, Knight, laird of Minto, hath taken possession in person in the summer of 1610; returned into Scotland; has nothing done. John Crawford, laird Kilberry, 1,000 acres; not appeared, nor any for him; nothing done. Alex. M'Aula, of Durlinge, 1,000 acres; appeared not; nothing done. Sir James Cunningham, Knight, laird Glangarnoth, 2,000 acres; took Possession, but returned into Scotland; his agent, Robert Younge, resident, built one Irish barn of coples; hath forty-four head of cattle, one plough of garrons, and some tillage last harvest. John Cunningham, of Crawfield, 1,000 acres; resident, with one family of British; is building a bawne and preparing materials; hath a plough of garrons, and thirty head of cattle. Cuthbert Cunningham, 1,000 acres; resident, with two families of British; built an Irish house of coples, and prepared materials to re-edify the Castle of Coole M'Ectrean; hath a plough of garrons, and eighty head of cattle in stock. William Stewart, laird of Dunduff, 1,000 acres; his brother was here for him in the summer of 1610, and returned into Scotland; left a servant to keep stock, being two mares and thirty head of cattle. James Cunningham, of Horomilne, 1,000 acres; was here in the summer of 1610, and returned into Scotland; left six servants to keep cows; nothing done; nor any preparations for building."

How the King raged over the foregoing and other similar reports implying such apathy on the part of his Scottish subjects! He had taken great credit to himself that the Scots had been permitted to plant in Ulster side by side with his English subjects, and now here was the result — this beggarly commencement, after a whole year's waiting and watching for better things from them. James had especially invited them to share in the Ulster spoils, thus:—"Forasmeikle as the King's Majesty having resolved to reduce and settle under a perfect obedience the North part of the kingdom of Ireland, which now, by the providence of the Almighty God, and by the power and strength of his Majesty's Royal army, is freed and disburdened of the former rebellious and disobedient inhabitants thereof, who in the justice of God, to their shame and confusion, are overthrown, his Majesty, for this effect, has taken a very princely and good course, as well for establishing of religion, justice, and civility within the said bounds, as for the planting of colonies therein; and, although there be no want of great numbers of the country people of England who with all gladness would transport themselves and their families to Ireland and plenish the whole bounds sufficiently with inhabitants, yet his Majesty, out of his unspeakable love and tender affection towards his ancient and native subjects, whom his Highness would have to partake in the fortunes of his said English subjects, has been pleased to make choice of them to be partakers in the distribution aforesaid." But the fact was that the Scottishmen, whether as planters or settlers, were not enthusiastic for the first year ; but when it was discovered that, on harvesting the first year's grain in Ulster, the settlers had not only enough for themselves, but could sell corn to their former neighbours in Scotland at a cheaper rate than the latter could raise it there, there arose over all the "land of mountain and of flood, of brown heath and shaggy wood," a fervid loyalty to the King, and love for the risk and labour of civilising the wild Irish—or such of them as had escaped the wrath of God, or rather the raiding of cruel and licentious Englishmen.

III.

The planters in Portlough were, with perhaps one exception, certain scattered members—*disjecta membra*—of the two great families of Stewart and Cunningham. 1. The duke of Lennox belonged to that branch of the Stewarts from which came also the Earls of March, the Earls and Dukes of Richmond, and the Earls of Litchfield. This undertaker of lands in Donegal was Ludovic Stuart, the second duke of Lennox, born in 1574, and during his life, which ended in 1624, enjoying several high offices of State. He accompanied the King to England in 1603, and thereupon became Master of the Royal Household and first Gentleman of the Bedchamber. He was afterwards created Earl of Newcastle and Duke of Richmond. Although thrice married he left no male heir, and thus the family estates devolved upon his brother Esme Stuart, who was known as Lord D'Aubigny—a title which had been introduced into the family by a former member of it, who had been so styled in right of his wife, the daughter of a French nobleman named De la Verray, Lord of Aubigny. The Duke of Lennox took out his patent among the first of the undertakers in this precinct, and it is a proof of how intensely the King had set himself to forward this plantation scheme when he induced persons of such high rank to be concerned in it only by way of example for the encouragement of others. Lennox was appropriately placed in three proportions which had all been intimately associated with the history of the O'Donnel family—and indeed one of these proportions contained the residence of the last chieftain's mother, from which she had been only recently expelled. Magevelin, one of the proportions allotted to the Duke, had been occupied until 1608 by the heroine known as Ineen-duv Macdonnell, a niece of the fourth Earl of Argyle, and mother of the Earl of Tyrconnell. These three proportions allotted to the Duke of Lennox came, as will be afterwards seen, into the hands of a turbulent relative known as Sir John Stewart.

The second on this list of Portlough planters was Sir Walter Stewart, laird of Minto, whose hold on his family property in the parish of Minto had become loose and uncertain. His native parish lies partly in a level tract along the River Teviot and partly on high undulating ground which is traversed from east to west by a ridge of hills culminating in two green rounded elevations, known as the Minto Hills, and overlooking the valley of the Teviot. Like so many other undertakers, Laird Minto came and got a proportion that after getting out his patent he might be able "to raise the wind"—*i.e.*, supply himself with a little needful cash by the prompt disposal of it to someone else more in love with land than himself. Accordingly his proportion of Coregagh soon became the property of Sir John Colquhoun, the laird of Luss, and the representative of a very old and very well known clan whose country lay on the banks of Loch Lomond. Sir John sold these lands afterward to two brothers, named Humphrey and Robert Galbraith, whose business transactions with Bishop Spottiswoode, of Clogher, as his agent, created so much noise in Tyrone and Donegal. Sir John Colquhoun's son eventually purchased back this proportion from the Galbraiths. 3. Alex. M'Aula, of Durling, is named by Pynnar Alex. M'Awley, *alias* Stewart, who sold his proportion to another Alex. Stewart, probably a near kinsman. The Earls and Marquises of Londonderry descend from the latter, their pedigree explaining the family by the introduction of a laird of Minto as their ancestor. That pedigree, as given in Burke's Peerage, and as probably supplied by some member of the family, states that they "claim a common ancestor with the Earls of Galloway—namely, Sir William Stewart, of Garlies, from whose second son, Thomas Stewart, of Minto, descended John Stewart, of Ballylawn Castle, the first [son of the first] of the family who settled in Ireland." John Stewart here mentioned was son of Alexander who bought the proportion called Ballyneagh from Alexander M'Aula, *alias* Stewart. In 1629 a Crown grant of the premises was made to this John Stewart, the lands being created into a manor to be called the manor of Stewarts-court. Ballylawn, the more modern name of the family residence, is a slight alteration from Ballyloane—the name of one sub-division on the estate. The fourth on the list of Portlough planters was John Cunningham, of Crawfield, the last representative of the Glengarnock Cunninghams in Scotland, his father, Sir James, and this son John, having both settled permanently in Donegal. The family residence of Glengarnock was situated in the parish of Kilbernie, Ayrshire, and this John Cunningham's property lay in the parish of Beith, also in the County of Ayr. After coming to his proportion of Dunboy, in Portlough, he continued to hold Crawfield until the year 1632, when it was sold to Gabriel Porterfield, of Hapland, in the parish of Dunlop, and Jean Maxwell, his spouse. The deed of sale was dated at Castle Cunningham, the residence of John Cunningham, of Dunboy, in the barony of Raphoe. His proportion was also known as Ardrie, both being names of parcels of land on the estate. In 1614 John Cunningham, afterwards Sir John, leased his lands to James Robin, Robert Hunter, John Martin, James Patterson, Alex. MacKilchany, John Plowright, John Molsed, Robert Allan, John Fyeff, Donnell M'Kilmun, John Wilson, Bernard Cunningham, James Boyle, John Bryce, William Sayer, or Sare, Donnell Gillaspick, John Fleming, Donnell M'Evene, William M'Cassack, Alex. Colewell, John Wigton, James Ramsay, Stephen Woolsen, Andrew Calwell, William Cunningham, Andrew Cunningham, Robert Boyle, and Donnell Connell.

The next, or fifth, planter on our list in this precinct was William Stewart, laird of Dunduff, who came from Maybole, in Ayrshire. The family to which he belonged was sometimes named Dunduff and sometimes Stewart. Although styled a laird, he was perhaps not more than able to gather up as much means as served to settle him on his proportion of Cooleaghy, in Portlough. The little property of Dunduff was sold to a family of the Whitefords in the neighbourhood. In 1614 the laird of Dunduff let lands on his proportion to the following tenants—viz., Archibald Thomson, John Coningham, John Hood, James Dunsayer, William Fullerton, Gilbert Kennedy, John M'Kay, John Smyth, Alex. Lokhard, Alexander Hunter, James Sayer, Walter Stewart, William Smelly, Thomas Lodge, Arthur Stewart, gent.; John Maghan, and

Anthony Stewart, gent. In 1829 the laird got a new grant from the Crown of all his land, the premises being created a manor, to be called the manor of Mountstewart. 6. Sir James Cunningham, laird of Glengarnock, who obtained two proportions, named respectively Dacrostross and Portelogh, was the eighteenth laird in descent from Sir Edward Cunningham, of Kilmaurs, and Mary Stewart, a daughter of the High Steward of Scotland. The general rental of Sir James Cunningham's barony of Glengarnock was £2,480, besides fifty-two bolls of meal, fourteen bolls of malt, twenty-four dozen and a half of capons, with work from the tenants sufficient to plow, harrow, weed, shear, draw in, and stack twenty-five acres of grain. But, with all these payments and this gratuitous help from others, his affairs had become desperate, and there was nothing for it but a permanent sojourn in Donegal. His lady was Kathrine Cunningham, a daughter of the Earl of Glencairn, and their family on coming to Donegal consisted of two daughters and a son, who were left quite unprovided for at the time of their father's death. The King interposed, and took a rather curious way of relieving them and paying any debts left by the deceased Sir James. The King simply ordered an Inquisition to find out whether all the conditions of plantation had been fulfilled in respect to his two proportions, and, when it was found that such was not the case, his Majesty refused pointblank to give any title to his creditors, who had got his lands, until ample provision had been made for his lady and family. 7. Cuthbert Cunningham was a brother of Sir James, of Glengarnock, but he either died soon after taking possession of his proportion called Dromagh, or returned to Ayrshire. Sir James was left in possession of these lands also, although quite ableun to manage his own. Indeed, he resided on this proportion of Dromagh, and died there in 1623, his son being then only nine years of age. 8. James Cunningham, Esq., was uncle of Sir James, of Glenarnock, and was known as of Fowmilne, in Scotland. He let his lands, known as the manor of Moiagh or Moyegh, to the following tenants in 1613—viz., Alexander Dunne, John Dunne, Donnll M'Kym, John Dunne, junior; John Younge, William Hendry, Alexander Grinney, William Stewart, William Valentyne, Hugh Moore, William Moore, David Kennedy, John Watson, Robert Paterson, William Aikin, George Blacke, Andrew Smyth, James Gilmore, William Gault, George Pery, John M'Kym, Andrew Browne, William Sutherland, William Rankine, John Smyth, John Purveyance, John Harper, Hugh Lokard, Thomas Scott, John Browne, John Roger, William Teyee, Donnell M'Eredy, William Arnett, Andrew Arnett, John Alexander, John Hutchine, Peter Stevenson, John Hamilton, Edward Homes, and George Leich. 9. Sir John Stewart was an agent for the Duke of Lennox, and also a kinsman, and held a proportion called Liemolmoghan on his own account. He appears to have been an unfaithful steward in more ways than one. The following letter from the King to the Lord Deputy Falkland, in 1628, throws some light on this case :—

"Whereas we have directed you by our letters to make a grant unto Sir James Fullerton and Sir David Murray of the several proportions of Magevelin, Lettergull, and Cashel, and sundry other lands and hereditaments, in trust and confidence to the only use and behoof of James, Duke of Lennox and Earl of March, forasmuch as Sir John Steward, who hath hitherto held possession of the aforesaid proportions, hath lately, in our realme of Scotland, been convicted of certain capital crimes, according to the laws of that our kingdom, for which he remains in prison there at our mercy for his life, we require you forthwith to give effectual order and warrant that the house and castle of Magevelin be delivered into the possession of

Thomas Holmes, agent there for our cousin, and that all the household stuff and utensils therein remaining, and the cattle on the ground lately belonging to the said Sir John Steward, be duly inventoried and put into the hands of the said Holmes until we give further direction therein. And, understanding that one William Yong, late servant to Sir John Steward, is fled into that kingdom, and hath carried with him several evidences, writings, and papers, and some plate, money, and jewels, lately belonging to Sir John, and further, that he is in that kingdom suspected of theft, and become a fugitive, it is our pleasure that you cause speedy and deligent search to be made after the said Yong, and, having found him, to cause such things of the nature aforesaid as can be discovered in his custody to be seized on, and the same to be put into the hands of some sufficient person until further disposing of of the the same; and likewise to commit him to prison, and, so soon as may be, to cause him to be sent in safe custody to our Council in Scotland, and there to undergo such trial as shall be thought fit."

From the precinct of Portlough the Commissioners of plantation passed into that of Boylagh and Bannagh, where the surveyors found 10,000 arable acres, which quantity was marked off into eight proportions and afterwards distributed amongst eight Scottish undertakers. The names of these North Britons were—Sir Robert Macklellan, laird of Bomby; George Murray, laird of Broughton; William Stewart Esq.; Sir Patrick M'Kee, of Laerg, Knight; James M'Cullock, gent.; Alexander Dunbar, gent.; Patrick Vans, of Libragh, gent.; and Alexander Coningham, of Powton, gent. The precinct of Boylagh and Bannagh, in which these planters were located, now forms the two baronies so-called, so that there was here vast scope around the 10,000 acres arable for improvement and augmentation. The barony of Boylagh contains 158,480 acres, including the district of the Rosses in the North, and twelve inhabited islands off the west coast. This barony comprehends part of the parishes of Inniskeel and Lower Killybegs, and the whole of the parishes of Lettermacward and Templecroan, its chief villages being Glenties and Dungloe. The barony of Bannagh contains 177,822 acres, including part of the parishes of Inniskeel and Lower Killybegs, and the parishes of Glencolumbkill, Inver, Kilcarr, Killoghtee, Upper Killybegs, and Killymard. Its towns and villages are Killybegs, Ardara, and Mountcharles. Much of the surface in this precinct still remains and ever will remain unprofitable.

IV.

Sir George Carew, in 1611, and after the planters last-named had been in possession for somewhat over twelve months, made the following report:—"Sir Robert Maclellan, Knight, laird of Bomby, chief undertaker of the Rosses, 2,000 acres; took possession in the summer 1610; returned into Scotland; his agent, Andrew Johnson, resident, has prepared no materials for building. George Murrye, laird Broughton, 1,500 acres; took possession summer 1610; returned into Scotland; his brother came with two or three others, and thirty or forty cows; no preparation for building. William Steward, brother to Gartlesse [Lord Garlies], 1,500 acres; took possession in the summer 1610; returned into Scotland; six families British upon his proportion; he is building a mill and other houses; agent, John Stewart, resident; materials provided for building. Sir Patrick M'Kee, Knight, 1,000 acres; not appeared; agent resident; nothing done. Alexander Cunningham, of Ponton, 1,000 acres; not appeared; agent resident; making winter provisions; no materials for building. James M'Cullogh, 1,000 acres; not appeared; agent resident; nothing done. Alexander Downbar, 1,000 acres; resident in person; nothing done. Patrick Vans, or Vance, 1,000; has not appeared; six quarters of his land let to English and Scotch men for four years; nothing done. George Murrye, laird Broughton, undertaker of 1,500 acres, appeared before us here at Dublin, and returned to his land."

The first and principal undertaker on the list of planters in the precinct of Boylagh and Bannagh was Sir Robert Maclellan, the seventh baron of Bombie, in Galloway, and afterwards created Lord Kircudbright. He became well known in Ulster, not so much, however, because of his being an undertaker in the remote barony of Boylagh as from the circumstance of his being son-in-law of Sir Hugh Montgomery, and obtaining valuable lands in the County of Down as his wife's dowry. The writer of the "Montgomery Manuscripts" notices this marriage alliance as follows:—"Sir Hugh married his eldest daughter to Sir Robert M'Clellan, baron of Kircoubry [Kircudbright], who, with her, had four great townlands near Lisnagarvey [Lisburn], whereof she was possessed in December, 1622. Sir Hugh and his Lady also had likewise given him a considerable sum of money as an augmentation to the marriage portion; but the said Sir Robert spent the money and sold the lands after her Ladyship's death, and he died not long after her, but without issue." In 1616 Sir Robert sold his proportion in Boylagh, called the Rosses, to Sir Archibald Acheson, who soon afterwards surrendered these lands to Sir John Murray, afterwards Earl of Annadale. 2. George Murray came from the parish of Whithorn, in Wigtonshire. The Murrays of this branch moved from Morayshire into Galloway in the twelfth century. From the commencement of the fifteenth century the Murrays were owners of the estate called Broughton, of which this

George Murray was at least the nominal owner when he came to Ulster. It had long been heavily mortgaged, and he, with his brother John, were taken in as servants in the Royal household. He soon disposed of his proportion called Boylagheightra. 3. William Stewart, Esq., was probably a servitor, but, as at this crisis there were four servitors so named, it would be difficult to identify this particular gentleman. A Colonel William Stewart, in May, 1603, writes privately to Salisbury that the "King's disposition is excellent, but he relies too much on others," and advises Cecil how to guide him "in this new world [England] to which he has come." Very soon after getting his patent this undertaker sold his proportion of Dunconnolly to Sir John Vance, of Lancaster, who appears to have lost it by neglecting to observe any of the conditions of plantation. 4. Sir Patrick M'Kee came from some place in the parish of Minnigaff, but the estate known as that of the principal family had passed out of his hands. Other localities were occupied by the once numerous and influential sept of the M'Kees, among which may be mentioned Mertoun-M'Kie, in the parish of Peninghame, and Whitehills, in the parish of Sorbie, Wigtonshire. Many settlers of this surname came to Ulster from Wigtonshire, and are numerously represented throughout several of our Northern counties at the present day. Sir Patrick let off his proportion of Cargie to William Stewart, of Maines, to his brother Patrick Stewart, of Raneall, and to Sir Robert Gordon.

The next, or fifth, on this list of grantees was James M'Cullock, who got a proportion named Mullaveagh, and had come also from Wigtonshire. His family had belonged to Argyleshire, and moved southward, like many other Northern families, into Galloway at an early period. This James was son of William M'Culloch, by his wife Elizabeth Dunbar, of Mocrum, a daughter of Elizabeth Muir, of Rowallan. In

1612 M'Culloch sold his lands of Mullaveagh to Patrick Nemoch, a burgess of Edinburgh. 6. Alexander Dunbar, gent., was a cousin to James M'Culloch, and came also from Galloway, where his family once occupied a leading position. This undertaker was a son of Sir John Dunbar, of Moorum, who died in 1583. He sold his proportion, called Kilkeran, to Sir Robert Gordon in 1615. 7. Patrick Vans, or Vance, gent., also came from Wigtonshire, where he owned a small property called Libragh, or Lybrack, in the parish of Kirkinner. He was the second son of Sir Patrick Vans, of Barnbarock, and his wife, Lady Cathrine Kennedy, daughter of Gilbert, third Earl of Cassilis. This family of Vans is said to be the only one in Galloway retaining its documents from the date of settlement in good preservation. Patrick Vans's patent was dated August 11, 1610,and he sold his proportion called Boylaghoutra to Patrick O'Murrey on the 3rd of October following. 8. Alexander Coningham came from the parish of Sorbie, in Wigtonshire, but to what branch of the then numerous race or clan bearing this surname he belonged we know not. The property of Poulton, or Powtoun, which he is stated in his grant as then holding, was conveyed in a charter given by King Robert Bruce to the prior of Whithorn. In a charter granted by David II. to Gilbert Kennedy, the lands of Powtoun are coupled with those of Carroltown, and are believed to have once formed part of that celebrated estate. Alexander Coningham sold his proportion called Moynarga to Sir Robert Gordon in 1615.

These Galloway gentlemen were specially unfortunate in their selection of Boylagh as their plantation precinct, for they must have had the selection of the barony, although they had to cast lots for the several proportions therein. They had evidently intended to plant in the same district, and were no doubt personally known to each other.

but the lines certainly had not fallen to them in pleasant places, and they appear to have made their way with becoming celerity from Donegal. The natives who had been dislodged or driven out in other quarters appear to have made their way more numerously to that place than the planters there could have wished, although the latter regarded it as a great grievance to be debarred altogether from employing Irish labourers. But Boylagh thus became a very decidedly congested district, and the wise King, the "Scottish Solomon," even with all the wisdom of his Council to back him up, could think of no remedy for the evil but force. At that time he had a prime favourite in John Murray, of Cockpool, who principally managed his private affairs in Scotland, and was supposed to be able to manage public affairs as well. So the grand idea was suggested, or was probably born in the Royal brain, that as these Boylagh undertakers could not manage their own affairs, and that as the original set had sold their proportions to persons even more incompetent than themselves, the latter should be required to surrender their lands, that the whole ten thousand acres which had been distributed amongst them might be granted to John Murray, who would be responsible for the peace of the district, and who would regrant their proportions to any planters wishing for repossession, and willing to carry out the conditions of plantation vigorously and rigorously. This scheme was carried out so far as the King and Council could do it; the grant was made to Murray, in 1620, "of all and every the several proportions and lands containing 10,000 acres, or thereabout, and lying in the barony or precinct of Boylagh and Bannagh." This arrangement did not mend matters much, if anything, and Murray, it was believed, required to be invested with additional powers. Accordingly, in 1625, as Earl of Annandale (he had been so dignified in

1624), he was appointed Governor of Donegal, and the borders and limits thereof, to suppress and punish by fire and sword malefactors, traitors, rebels, and all who refuse to submit to the law. The King did not live to see how futile was his attempted government by force, or to be convinced of the cruelty and injustice of his policy towards the native inhabitants of Ulster.

The two plantation precincts set apart in Donegal for servitors and natives were Doe and Farnaght—two Irish territories the names of which have now become almost obsolete. These two divisions of ancient Tyrconnell form the barony of Kilmacrenan, Fanaght, or Fannat, being the eastern portion of the barony, and Doe, lying along the western coast, is nearly comprised in the present parish of Clondehorkey. Kilmacrenan contains 310,656 acres, including part of the parish of Conwall with the whole parishes of Aughanuncheon, Aughnish, Clondehorkey, Clondevaddock, Garton, Kilgarvan, Kilmacrenan, Mevagh, Raymunterdony, Tullaghobegley, and Tullyfern. The towns and chief villages in this barony are Letterkenny, Ramelton, Dunfanaghy, Doaghbeg, Rathmullan, Creeslough, Ballyroosky, and Tawny. The Commissioners found 12,500 arable acres in the precinct of Doe, and 13,000 in the precinct of Fanaght, and these two quantities were marked of into twenty proportions. The two remaining baronies of Inishowen and Tirhugh were not given to undertakers—the former, as already mentioned, being handed over to Chichester, and the latter, which only had 4,000 acres arable, allotted to Trinity College, Dublin. From the camp at Lifford, Davys wrote to Salisbury, on the 12th of September, after having, as he believed, finished the work in Donegal to perfection:—"We are now come," says Davys, "to the tropic or turning point of our journey; for, having finished the services which were to be performed in Tyrconnell, we begin to return homewards from hence to Fermanagh, from thence to Cavan, where we will make the last period of this summer's progress or circuit. Divers persons have exhibited their pretended titles to land in this country [Donegal], whereof some are merchants of the Pale, to whom the late fugitive Earl of Tyrconnell [Rorie O'Donnell] had mortgaged great scopes of land for small sums of money; others are natives, who, being chiefs of septs, suppose their long continuance of possession under O'Donnell to be a good title now against the Crown. Besides, some of their widows claim jointures and dowers, though, by their own Irish law, no woman may have any estate in the land. But all these titles appear to be void or voidable in English law, so that the pretenders [rather the only rightful owners] are left entirely to his Majesty's grace and bounty." The native chiefs of septs referred to by Davis were several named MacSwyne (now Sweeny)—viz., Donnell MacSwyne Fanett, Sir Mulmorie MacSwyne na Doe, Donaugh MacSwyne Banagh, Walter MacLaughlin MacSwyne, and Manus MacNeal MacSwyne, Tirlagh O'Boyle, whose ancestors were lords of Boylagh, and Hugh MacHugh Duff O'Donnell. Donough MacSwyne Banagh was the representative of the princely Niall Mor MacSwyne, whom the Four Masters describe, at the year 1524, as "a constable of hardiest hand and heroism, best in withholding and attacking, best in hospitality and prowess, who had the most numerous troops and the most vigorous soldiers, and who had forced the greatest number of passes of any man of his own fair tribe."

V.

The twenty proportions of arable land found in the two precincts of Doe and Fanaght, or in the barony of Kilmacrenan, were allotted, with some trifling exceptions, to the following servitors—viz., William Stewart, Esq.; Patrick Crawford, Esq.; John Vaughan, Esq; John Kingsmill, Esq.; Basill Brooke, Esq.; Sir Richard Hansard, Thomas Perkins, and George Hilton, gents.; Sir Thomas Chichester, knight; Henry Hart, Esq; Sir Ralph Bingley, knight; Edward Ellis, gent.; Henry Vaughan, Esq.; Sir Richard Bingley, of Westminster, knight; George Gale, gent.; Charles Grimsditche, gent.; and Thomas Browne, Esq. Sir George Carew sent the following short report from what he called the precinct of Kilmacrenan in 1611:—"Captain William Stewart has built upon the proportion of 1,000 acres, granted to him as a servitor, a fort, or bawne, of lime and stone, with two flankers. Under one is a room either for a munition house or a prison, and upon that a court of guard, and above that an open feight, and in the outmost part thereof a centinel house, one curtain sixteen foot high, and two others twelve foot high, and the other eight foot high, whereupon he intends to erect a stone house; has built three houses, English fashion, and is in hand for more, which will serve for tenants. The rest of the servitors have done nothing by reason of the wildness of the land, being the worst in all the country, insomuch that the natives are unwilling to come to dwell upon it until they be forced to remove. Servitors are providing materials and purpose to perform their covenants by the time prescribed. Tyrlagh O'Boyle, with tenants and followers, removed to the proportion assigned to him in the said barony. M'Swyne Bannagh will remove to his proportion, but in the meantime he and his followers have bought grazing of Alexander Kernes, general agent for the Scottish undertakers in the precinct of Boylagh and Bannaght. Said natives have performed no works, but are providing materials; none others have removed to portions assigned."

The planters in Kilmacrenan had ample

grounds for their slow, and in most cases no progress, during their first year of occupancy. 1. This William Stewart came from the parish of Whithorn, Wigtonshire, the lands there belonging to his family being known as Barclay, Castlewigg, and Tanderagie. This branch of the Stewarts was founded by Walter Stewart of the Garlies family, and we have already had some references to the career of Sir William—perhaps its most distinguished member—in connection with the town of Newtonstewart. In addition to all the lands he had obtained by plantation grants in the baronies of Strabane and Kilmacrenan, he received a grant, in conjunction with Sir Henry Tichburne, of all the rents, profits, and forfeitures of sundry lands in Ulster which had escheated to the Crown because of being set by planters to the native Irish, contrary to the conditions in their patents, to be held during pleasure, towards satisfaction of all arrears of pay due to them (Stewart and Tichburne) and their soldiers from the Crown, since their employment in Ireland, until Michaelmas, 1629. In 1638 he purchased extensive lands in the barony of Omagh also, thus laying the foundations of a family, broad and deep, whose representatives became Viscounts Mountjoy and Earls of Blessington. 2. Patrick Crawford, of Lifford, Esq., belonged to a Scottish family which had settled in Donegal at the time of Ineenduv Macdonnell's marriage with the chieftain of Tyrconnell. This Patrick Crawford's father, Owen, or John, Crawford, was living in 1610 near the town of Donegal, and his brother David was an attendant on the Earl of Tyrconnell when the latter made his escape with the Earl of Tyrone in the autumn of 1607. Captain Patrick Crawford was appointed to accompany Sir Oliver Lambert in an expedition against Dunyveg, in Isla, and fell at the siege of that fortress, February, 1613-14. Lambert, when writing to the King an account of the expedition, concludes his letter in the following terms :—"Your Majesty has lost, in the death of Captain Graifford, a valiant captain by whom I was not a little assisted. The fortune of war is not to be resisted." Crawford's widow married Sir George Marburie, or Malbury, who soon afterwards got out a patent for Crawford's proportion of Letterkenny in right of his wife. Malbury was one of Sir Richard Hansard's executors.

The next, and third, planter on the foregoing list was John Vaughan, Esq , who sold his proportion of Carnagilly soon after visiting the same to John Wray. He did not, however, leave the district, but accepted the very dangerous office of High Sheriff for Donegal. In May, 1610, a Mr. Fox, writing from Dublin to Salisbury, mentions a report then in circulation "of the killing of Captain John Vaughan, the Sheriff of the County of Dunnagall, by a Scotchman, upon a sudden falling out between them." There were many Scotchmen crowding into that county at the date above-mentioned who would have made short work with sheriffs had circumstances called for the practical use of the dirk ; but the rumour in this case was exaggerated, for Vaughan survived the assault, was afterwards created a knight, admitted a member of the Privy Council, and appointed Governor of the city of Londonderry. His daughter and heir, Sidney Vaughan, married Sir Frederick Hamilton, youngest son of Lord Paisly, who followed his brothers to Ulster, and whose representatives were ennobled as Viscounts Boyne. 4. John Kingsmill, Esq., was the son of Sir William Kingsmill, keeper of Freemantle Park, Hampshire, an office which a younger son, Henry, had in reversion. Another brother named Andrew received £170 for his interest in certain coppices in Finkley Walk, Forest of Chute, Hampshire, purchased by the King for the preservation of deer. Sir John's proportion of Ballymally, in Kilmacrenan, remained comparatively waste even at the date of Pynnar's survey, 1618-20. 5.

Basill Brooke, Esq., had distinguished himself as a servitor in Ireland, and was one of those selected by the King for a proportion of land in the Ulster plantation. He was soon afterwards knighted, and was styled as of Magherabegg and Brook Manor, in the County of Donegal. He married Anne, daughter of Thomas Leicester, of Toft, in the County of Chester, and died in 1633. His son and heir was Sir Henry Brooke, of Brooksborough, in the County Fermanagh. Brook Manor was also known as Killydonnell, and Pynnar called Basill Brooke's proportion Edoncarne. 6. Sir Richard Hansard was among the most useful and energetic of the servitor class, and yet he does not appear to have been rewarded for his services—at least on the same liberal scale as others, who were not perhaps so deserving. In addition to his dignity of knighthood, he got only a comparatively small grant at Lifford, and even this was accompanied with certain stringent conditions. It is stated in substance as follows in the Patent Rolls :—"The town of Liffer, or Ballyduffe, one quarter ; Killenederiogh, one quarter ; Croghan and Shanden, one quarter ; Cabragh, one quarter, with the ferry over the Finn, between Liffer and Strabane, and power to erect one or more ferries over the River Deale [Derg] between the lands of Liffer and Conleigh. From this grant were excepted the fort known as Captain Brooke's Fort, to be called the King's fort, and the meadow of Stramore, near Liffer, except four acres thereof in the north-east point to be reserved to Sir Richard, with fishing in the Finn."

The next, or seventh, on the foregoing list were George Hilton and Thomas Perkins, gents., but why these undertakers were thus associated in so small a quantity of land as 300 acres we cannot explain. Thomas Perkins is styled Lieutenant Parkins in another plantation document. He is mentioned in an inquisition as one of Sir Richard Hansard's executors. George Hilton is also mentioned in an inquisition as renting a part of the quarter of Garwery, in the proportion of Shragmirlar, from Peter Benson, of London, who had purchased from Sir Henry Clare. 8. Sir Thomas Chichester was the youngest brother of the then Deputy, Sir Arthur Chichester, and, in common with some others, had expressed a wish to have his proportion near the borders of Inishowen, which belonged to Sir Arthur, and, as a matter of course, would be thoroughly protected against the native inhabitants. In the Deputy's instructions for the Treasurer going to London, January, 1609-10, he says :— "Sir Thomas Chichester and others seek for lands about those parts, because it joins so near my land of Inishowen more than for the goodness of the soil." But Sir Thomas was already provided with rich and broad lands in the County of Wicklow, although he dwelt in Inishowen, perhaps in the capacity of agent for his brother. His place of residence there was Birte, or Burte, Castle, which had belonged to Sir Cahir O'Dogherty. In it Sir Thomas Chichester died on the 20th of August, 1616, and was succeeded by his son Charles, who was of age and unmarried at the date of his father's death. 9. Henry Hart, so well known in connection with Sir Cahir O'Dogherty's revolt, belonged to an English Roman Catholic family. In February, 1604-5, he was appointed constable or keeper of the castle and fort of Culmore, with 300 acres adjoining, including all fishings and other appurtenances as reserved to the Crown in the letters patent made to Sir Cahir O'Dogherty, the grantee being required to search all shipping coming to the ports of Lough Foyle and the Derrie for munition, armour, and all other prohibited wares and merchandises imported or exported out of the same; provided the said Harte shall not use any unnecessary vexations to the King's subjects, or others in amity with his Majesty, coming to trade and traffic in those parts of Ulster. In the spring of 1608 Harte was seized by O'Dogherty, who compelled him to give up Culmore; and, although he was in no way to blame for the surprise, he appears to have been suspected by some people for connivance in the affair. The whole series of disastrous events, however, arising from that surprise ended in securing the barony of Inishowen for Chichester, and the latter may have felt so much obliged to Harte, whether conniving or faithful, that he was put on the list of servitors considered suitable for undertakers. He therefore got the proportion of 1,000 acres called Ballynae, with 256 acres of concealments. In an inquisition of 1661 Henry Harte is styled of Muffe, and is also therein stated to have sold to Wybrant Olphert, for the sum of £300, the several quarters of land called Inisbofin, Maghreyoutra, Ballanae, Balleconnell, Drumnalumney, Ardbegg, Ardmore, and Gortcarke, in the barony of Kilmacrenan.

The next, or tenth, servitor on this list of undertakers was Sir Richard Bingley, probably a brother of Sir Ralph Bingley—or perhaps Richard is a misprint for Ralph. At all events, when Pynnar inspected, 1618 20, Captain Sanford held Doe Castle, which had been "the strongest hold in all the province," with 500 acres of Bingley's proportion. Of this knight we have already heard in connection with the proportions of Tawnaforis, Drummore, and Lurga. 11. Edward Ellis's name is generally written Edmund in plantation papers. He sold his lands to Edward Rowley, who died in 1641, and was succeeded by his son and heir, Sir John Rowley, who was 27 years of age at the date of his father's death. 12. Henry Vaughan was a brother to Sir John above mentioned. 13. George Gale, gent., appears to have held but a small portion as a servitor. He died in 1628, leaving two daughters, Eliza and Margaret—the one four years of age and the other two years at the time of their father's death. In 1642 Eliza was 18 years old, and had married William Hamilton; and her sister Margaret was then 16, and had married Francis Hamilton 13. Charles Grimsditch, gent., was brother of a John Grimsditch who, n 1604, had a Royal grant in reversion, after Bristow Pigeon, of the keeping of the King's wardrobe in the Tower, and of the garden there, for life. 14. Thomas Brown is sometimes mentioned in the "Domestic Series of State Papers" as a sort of surveyor, who seems to have become rather troublesome to Salisbury by the too frequent application for little favours. Amongst other matters, Browne wrote to the Prime Minister asking "confirmation" of the bailiwick of Pinchbeck, granted him by the late Lord Burghley, Salisbury's father. The surveyor, however, does not appear to have prospered in that suit, for he wrote soon again stating that he "had heard that the bailiwick of Pinchbeck had been conferred on another," and urging his own prior right to it. This grant to Browne, in Ulster, of 528 acres may have very probably been made to compensate him for disappointments elsewhere. He got his new premises created the manor of Brownstowne, with 200 acres in demesne, and a court baron.

VI.

Several natives in Donegal got small grants, but most of the leading families there had been swept away during the terrible war between the Government and the Northern Earls. Among the State papers of the reign of James I. is the following curious and historically important document recording the names and places of residence of such old Irish families of rank as dwelt westward of Lough Swilly:— "From the entrie of the Lough [Swilly] untill you come to a point of land a little short of Ench [island of Inch] there is neither castle nor fort; but then upon a poynt of lande is a castle and an abbey called Ramullan [now Rathmullen] —MacSwyne O'Farre's [O'Fanaid's] chiefe country-house. Fyve miles above Ramullan there is a castle of Hugh MacHugh Duffe's [O'Donnell's], called Ramalton, standing upon the Lannan [the River Lenan], which falleth in Lough Swilly—Hugh Duffe's own house. Three miles above Ramalton, upon the lough side, in a baye, is the Abbey of Kil-O'Donnell, in Hugh MacHugh Duffe's countrey. Here dwell only fryers. Fyve miles above Kil-O'Donnell there is a ford, passable at low water, wherein hath sometime been a forte, called the Farcet [Fearsad] of Soloughmore. Three myles from this ford, towards Birt, stands an abbey called Ballaghan, over against Kil-O'Donnell; here dwell fryers. Three myles from Ballaghan, towards Birt, is a poynt of land which runs farr into the lough, where hath bene a strong fort, but nowe broken downe, and is called Dunboy; here dwells Shane MacManus Oge [O'Donnell]. Dunboye and the poynt of lande whereon Birte standeth maketh a baye, in the bottom whereof standeth an old forte called Cul MacTryen; this was wont to be held by O'Donnell. From Cul MacTryen runs a bogg three myles in length to the syde of Lough Foyle; in the midst of the bogg is a standing loughe, with a forte on the syde of the loughe called Bunneber [Bun-aber], where Alexander MacSorlie [son of Sorly Boy Macdonnell] was slain. At the end of this bogg, to Lough Foyle syde, is the fort of Cargan; here dwells O'Donnell's mother [Ineendubh Macdonnell]. Three myles above Cargan stands a fort call M'Gwyvelin [now Mongevlin], uppon the River of Lough Foyle—O'Donnell's mother's chiefe house. Above M'Gwyvelin, four myles up the River of Lough Foyle, is the Liffer; here dwelt [the] O'Donnell.

"Four myles above the Liffer stands Castle Fene [Fynne], Niall Garve's [O'Donnell's] house. Four myles above Castle Fene is a fryers' house called Drumboy. Three myles above Drumboy stands a fort called Ballakit; here dwells Donnell Gallocar [O'Gallagher], one of O'Donnell's chiefe counsellors. Ten myles above Ballakit is Loughfene [Fynne], upon the River Fene, where the river hath its first head. Four myles westward from Ballakit is Barnesmore. From Barnesmore to the Castle of Baleek, that standeth upon Lough Erne, is twelve myles. From Beleek to Ballashanan is three myles. Here dwells M'O'Dungourye. From Ballashanan to the Abbey of Asheroe, to the seawards, is one myle; inhabited by monks. From the Abbey of Asheroe to the Abbey and Castle of Dunagall is nyne myles. Here is a good haven, and the River Eske falls into it. Three myles above Dunagall is Lough Eske—O'Donnell's chiefe keeping, O'Donnell's chiefe storehous for the warr. Over against Dunagall, two myles on the other syde of the water, stand O'Boyle, where the ships used to ride—O'Boyle's chiefe house. Seven myles from O'Boyle, to the seaward, is a castle called M'Swyn O'Bane's [Bannagh's] Tower. From this place to the haven of Calboy (Killybegs) is three miles—here dwells Seneschall M'Gonell. Four myles from there stands the Castle of Bromoyle—in the lower end of the countrey—here dwells Hugh boy M'Swyne O'Bane's brother. From thens four myles is a small haven called Cornetillen. This haven divydes M'Swyne O'Bayne's countrey and O'Boyle's. At the lower end of O'Boyle's country is a castle called Kilmirrish. Here dwells the Bishop of O'Boyle. Next to that castle is the haven of Bonabbar. This haven parteth O'Boyle's countrey and M'Swyne O'Doe's. And next to that is the haven Conogarhen, with a castle so called; this is M'Swyne O'Doe's chiefe house. The next haven to this is Red Haven, which parteth M'Swyne O'Doe's country and M'Swyne O'Fane's [Fanet's]. By the syde of this haven is the Castle of Menryee, a castle of M'Swyne O'Fanet's.

Small boats may come from the Red Haven to the castle. Here dwells Alexander M'Donologhe. The midland of Tyrconnell is inhabited by the sept of O'Gallocars."

Several districts in Donegal were known as the waste lands of the Clann-Dalaigh, or O'Donnells, where the chief had always the privilege of placing his fuidher, or fugitives, "stranger-tenants"—to him a very important class. These were outlaws or fugitives from other tribes who came to him for protection, and who were only connected with the Clann-Dalaigh by their dependence on the chief—being simply groups or companies collected from other territories, and calling themselves tribesmen, but in reality associations formed by contract among themselves, and chiefly for the purpose of pasturing cattle. This comparatively despised class were exposed to the frequent exactions of the chief when his necessities became pressing; they were really the first *tenants-at-will* known in Ireland, and were always rack-rentable when circumstances required. They were not, however, in other respects oppressively treated by the chief on whose lands they took up their abode, for it was really his interest to encourage them, and by their willingness to work and pay they generally became sources of his wealth. The members of the regular clan invariably looked on these *fuidher* with jealous feelings, their own interests, as they believed, always suffering in proportion to the curtailment of such waste lands as had been used by themselves for purposes of fuel and pasture.

Only forty natives in the whole extensive County of Donegal obtained small grants in the dreary regions of Doe and Fanet, now Kilmacrenan. Several of them were representatives of noble Irish families, and the remainder belonged to the class of native gentry. The prevailing surnames amongst them were those of O'Donnell, MacSwyne, O'Gallagher, and O'Boyle. A few very old people got pretty liberal grants, but with remainders to Sir Ralph Bingley and Sir Richard Hansard.

Bishop George Montgomery was one of the King's most active agents in the work of plantation, and had ample field for the exercise of all his powers in this project, for he held no fewer than three bishopricks at one and the same time—those of Clogher, Derry, and Raphoe. He had thus enormous revenues, but he was, nevertheless, sadly disappointed that he could not get hold of all the harenagh lands—and they were very extensive — throughout his three dioceses. He argued that all harenagh lands should belong to the Church, but Davys and Chichester thought otherwise, and accordingly claimed them for the Crown. He had enough on hands without them, and he spared no pains to induce Scottish settlers to come to his assistance. His grand-nephew, William Montgomery of the "Manuscripts," has rendered due homage to the Bishop's zeal in this matter of plantation. "Now," says he, "as to his Lordship's usefulness in advancing the British plantation in those three Northern dioceses, the footsteps [footprints] of his so doing are yet visible; so that I need but tell the reader that he was very watchful, and settled intelligences to be given from all the seaports in Donegal and Fermanagh, himself most residing at Derry, but when he went to view and lease the Bishop's lands, or settled preachers in parishes, of which he was very careful. The ports resorted to from Scotland were Derry, Donegal, and Killybegs; to which places the most that came were from Glasgow, Ayr, Irwin, Greenock, and Largs, and places from within a few miles from Braidstane [the Bishop's native place]; and he ordered so that the masters of vessels should, before dislodging their cargoes, which were for the most part meal and oats, come to his Lordship with a list of their seamen and passengers. The vessels stayed not for a market. He was their merchant and encourager to traffic in those parts, and wrote to that effect, as also to the said towns wherein he was much acquainted and esteemed; and had proclamations made in them all at how easy rents he would let his Church lands, which drew thither many families, amongst whom, one Hugh Montgomery, his kinsman, a master of a vessel, and also owner, who brought his wife and children and effects, and were settled at Derrybroek, near Enniskillen, where his son Nicholas, my long acquaintance, aged about eighty-five years, now lives in sound memory, and is a rational man, whose help I now want to recount particulars of that Bishop's proceedings in that country whilst his Lordship stayed there, which was at least, till near Anno 1618. One other Montgomery, named Alexander, a minister, his Lordship settled near Derry. He was prebend of Doe, and lived until about 1658. Thus, by the Bishop George's industry, in a few years the plantation was forwarded, and Church revenues increased greatly. I was credibly told that for the encouragement of planters [tenant-settlers] on Church lands he obtained the King's orders to the governors, and an Act of Council thereon, that all the leases he made, which were for thirty-one years, should not be taken from the planters [tenant-settlers] or their posterity at the expiration of their term, but renewed to them as they held the same, they paying their bishop one year's rent for renewal of their leases to the other thirty-one years—which was a very encouraging certainty—but the Parliament since that time have taken other measures more for bishops' than tenants' profits."

THE COUNTY OF FERMANAGH.

I.

In bringing all the temporal lands in Fermanagh to the Crown, and consequently into the vast field for plantation, there were certain difficult questions to be discussed and determined. Sir Hugh Maguire was the representative of a long line of Clann-Colla chieftains, or toparchs, reaching from the seventh to the seventeenth century, and was very popular throughout all his "country" of Fermanagh. He married a daughter of the Earl of Tyrone, and became one of the ablest and most trusted leaders in the war of the Northern Lords against the Government. He fell in battle, and Queen Elizabeth, in her wrath, hastily had his entire territory of Fermanagh confiscated and handed over to his cousin, Connor Roe Maguire, who had taken the side of the English in the war, and was known as Maguidir Gallda, or the "English Maguire." But this high-handed arrangement, which had been almost exclusively the work of the Queen, required to be set aside after her death, and the county was then divided into two nearly equal parts between Connor Roe and his cousin, Cuconaght Maguire, a younger brother of the deceased Sir Hugh. This arrangement, however, although so much more equitable than the former, failed to reconcile the rivals, or to give peace to the distracted clansmen. At length Cuconaght resolved to have no longer parley with his treacherous cousin, or with the Government who had set him up against the wishes of the clansmen. He had made up his mind to leave Ulster for some more congenial home on the Continent, and, on hearing that the Earls of Tyrone and Tyrconnell were about to sail from Loughswilly, he hastily joined them. The Four Masters refer briefly to the fate of Cuconaght Maguire, describing him as a "rapid-marching, adventurous man, endowed with wisdom and beauty of person." His "rapid-marching," however, was soon destined to come to an end on the Continent, for he died of fever on his arrival at Genoa.

His death, in part, relieved Chichester of a great difficulty which could not otherwise have been permanently removed; for how was Fermanagh to be secured for plantation if Cuconaght, a hostile chief, were permitted to hold the full half of the county—as had been regularly arranged by Sir George Carew, the deputy preceding Chichester? Cuconaght's portion, or half, included some of the most important positions in the county, and comprised the half barony of Coole, the whole baronies of Lurgue, Magheryboy, and Clinawley, with so much of the barony of Knockninny as lies on the southern and western shores of Lough Erne, together with such islands in the lough as anciently belonged to the several divisions now named. By this arrangement, Cuconaght also held of right the castle of Enniskillen, which was then considered the key to the whole district. In referring to that mode of settlement, Chichester explained his disapproval thereof in the following terms:—"For in certain instructions in the time of Sir George Carew's Government, his Highness [James I.] signified his express pleasure that the whole country should be divided between those two chieftains, without further limitation, according to which if it can be settled there can be little good hope that ever that country can come to civility and obedience, being left in a manner wholly to the self-willed government of those two chiefs." The problem, however, which thus seemed seriously to stand in the way was all but solved by the death of Cuconaght—an event, however, which Chichester simply regarded as so far so good—for what now was to be done about

Connor Roe's half of the county, or were the Commissioners of Plantation to be shut out from the two whole baronies of Magheristephana and Clancally, and from the half of the barony of Tyrcannada, and from the half of the barony of Knockninny?

But the astute Deputy was not so punctilious about little trifles of this nature as some others appear to have been. By the time the Commissioners were ready to commence operations in Fermanagh he had found a key for the lock that threatened to shut them out from Connor Roe's lands. "Connor Roe," writes Chichester to Salisbury, "expects to have three baronies, upon some promise made to him when the traitors Tyrone, Tyrconnell, and other Irish lords were restored to their lands; but a more prudent course being now in hand, I see not that the King is bound in honour to make so barbarous and unworthy a man greater than his neighbours, but rather, in true construction of State, to suppress him, for all his actions declare an ill mind, and I am sure he will do much harm to the plantation if he be made so great. The barony of Magheristephana will contain him and all his followers and goods that depend on him, and that quantity, in my opinion, is rather too much than too little for him." And, verily, after lengthened negotiations, and many distracting remonstrances on the part of Connor Roe, the whole affair came to this, that the "English Maguire," who had deserted his own people to fight for England during the war of seven years, was obliged to accept a much smaller portion than Magheristephana, and on the conditions by which other undertakers were bound. But even this was not all. On the allotment finally made to Maguire stood his old family residence of Lisnaskea, with its surrounding demesne, but the castle and lands had been granted away to a Scottish planter, named Lord Burley, during the delay caused by Connor Roe's remonstrances, and probably by some mistake in the measurements of the district. Burley would not waive his claim, and to have done with Maguire's case altogether Chichester proposed to get a pension for him, and let him clear out. In a list of propositions sent to the Council in London, one is "that Connor Roe M'Guire may have pension of £200 a year for life, which has been offered him. and £50 to one of his sons after his decease, for like term; to which he would not listen, but prepares to go over (to London) and be a further suitor to his Majesty for recompense of the three baronies and all the islands that were taken from him." To this proposition the Council replied that it was "reasonable, if it will be accepted by Connor Roe. If not, then the Lord Deputy and Council in Dublin are to establish and maintain the Lord Burley in the possession, leaving Connor Roe to take his remedy. For this there is likewise a letter procured from his Majesty." So, Maguire had no remedy but to clear out of his castle and its demesne lands, and be thankful to live with his pension (during the few years that then remained to him), on the other lands conveyed in his own grant.

The temporal lands in Fermanagh were thus brought, without any exceptions, to the Crown. The termon and herenagh lands were more extensive in this county than perhaps anywhere else throughout Ulster, and were eagerly claimed by the Protestant bishops for the Church, but in this their awfully clutching policy signally failed. The termon and herenagh lands, as already mentioned, originally belonged in part to the early Irish Church, but in later times it was found by the Commissioners that these lands had been owned for many centuries by the minor septs, or in other words by the clansmen, and, such being the case, the legal acumen of Davys, the Attorney-General, clearly demonstrated that every description of landed property in the hands of the people was confiscated, and as a matter of course belonged to the Crown. Thus all the lands in Fermanagh were prepared for plantation purposes, excepting some belonging to the Church, but even the new bishops themselves were held to the conditions of plantation. And there was, perhaps, no portion of Ulster more eagerly coveted by outsiders generally than Fermanagh, with its beauteous islands and its most picturesque shores on both sides of Lough Erne. So felt the Norsemen during their many and very unwelcome visits to Ulster, and so felt the undertakers from north and south of the Tweed, who rivalled each other in their efforts to get into that county, and who eventually shared its hills, and glades, and islands amongst them. Sir John Davys was not slow in recognising the natural beauties and advantages of Fermanagh. When writing to Salisbury, from Enniskillen, in the autumn of 1609, he says :— "We have now finished our service in Fermanagh, which is so pleasant and fruitful a country that if I should make a full description thereof it would rather be taken for a poetical fiction than a true and serious narration. The fresh lake called Lough Erne—being more than forty miles in length, and abounding in fresh water fish of all kinds, and containing one hundred dispersed islands—divides that country into two parts The land on either side of the lough, rising in little hills of eighty or a hundred acres apiece, is the fattest and richest soil in all Ulster."

These statements are generally correct, indeed surprisingly so, when it is considered how little time Davys had to make notes, and what heavy matters must have then been occupying his thoughts. He speaks only in general terms, however, as to the size of Lough Erne, the number of its islands, and the lands along its shores. The area of the upper lake is about 9,453 acres, and that of the lower lake about 27,645. Of this entire area the County Fermanagh has 36,348 acres, the County of Cavan about 749, and the County of Donegal only one acre and twenty-two perches. His description of the land as rising on each side in little hills may be accepted as generally accurate, for undulations, slopes, and gently-ascending hills form both the margin and skyline of the grand valley, although many delectable meadow-lands, "warm and low," broadly fringe the shores of the lakes, upper and lower. Instead of there being only forty-six islands in Lough Erne, as stated by the Plantation Commissioners, or one hundred islands, as Davys supposed, there are upwards of two hundred well known, and besides many smaller ones might be enumerated. The Commissioners, however, were looking about in the islands, as everywhere else in their perambulations, only for the arable acres ; and, on this errand bent, it was unnecessary to visit all the islands, for the lands really available for agricultural purposes do not comprise more than about 2,000 acres, and are found in only those of the larger size. Lough Erne consists, strictly speaking, of two parts, or rather two distinct and well-defined portions of the same, connected by a broad winding channel of six miles in length. The upper or southern portion of the lough is nine miles long, and from one and a half mile to five miles in breadth ; the lower, or northern, expanse of water, or that portion of the lough between Enniskillen and the sea, is ten miles long, and varies from two to eight miles in width. Both portions are crowded with islands, several of which are well wooded and inhabited. The upper part, reaching from Belturbet to Enniskillen, is so thickly studded with islands as to appear like a number of winding channels rather than a lough ; whilst the islands in the lower lake are not so numerous, and generally of greater individual extent. Among the islands up and down, here and there, occur fragments of the ancient cairn, the rath, the cromlech, the pillar-stone, the castle, and the abbey. With these curious remains of the past only one round tower lifts up its silent and mysterious face, and is said to be about the most interesting specimen of its class in Ireland. Lough Erne is celebrated as a retreat and shelter for birds in winter—these feathered visitors coming from the northern coasts of Antrim and even from the Scottish islands. The people dwelling on the islands are pretty much what we would expect to find in the remote and secluded nooks where they live—contemplative, peace-loving, passionately attached to their homes, and fond of cherishing such old traditions as still linger about the islands.

II.

THE whole area of Fermanagh comprises about 289,228 acres, of which there are now at least 115,000 arable. The county is divided into eight baronies—viz., Knockninny, Glenawley, and Magheraboy, on the left or west side of the lough; and on the right or east side are Coole, Clonkelly, Magherastephana, Tyrkennedy, and Lurg. The Commissioners of Plantation divided the county into eight precincts, the names of which were Glancally, Coolmakernan and Lurge, Knockninny, Magheriboy, Clanawley, Coole and Tyrcannada. Before they had time to commence operations in this county, a company of forty Englishmen came forward with a proposal to undertake for the whole lands of Fermanagh, to invest a sum of £40,000 in the speculation, to build forty manor houses therein, and to plant according to whatever conditions the authorities might recommend or impose. To this proposal they appended a request, as follows:—"The forty undertakers whose names are hereunder written are also petitioners for a grant of that small part of the County of Sligo now in the hands of the King, which lies between the end of Lough Erne and the sea; as they intend to have a market town on the south side thereof, at Belleek, and from thence, three miles nearer the sea, to erect a strong corporation. This part of Sligo contains about three miles, being a piece of ground very convenient, adjoining the sea, for the necessary use of the inhabitants of that corporation for bringing in or transporting their commodities." The Government did not intend to deal with undertakers in companies but as individuals; and, besides, it was not thought expedient to introduce so many landlords into Fermanagh, at least for a time. Although this company offered to appoint Sir Thomas Chichester, brother of Sir Arthur, as their leader, and to provide him with six assistants, the proposal fell through, and of the forty not more than four eventually obtained estates in this much coveted county.

Nor was the company of Dutchmen more fortunate in their application, about the same time, for a Crown grant of all the islands in Lough Erne. Indeed, they were hardly so much so, for not one of them appears to have got any lands at the general distribution afterwards, although Davys spoke of their application in highly recommendatory terms. In his glowing account of the scenery and soil of Fermanagh, from which we have already quoted, he makes a practical, although perhaps rather a novel, suggestion under the circumstances, as follows:—"Here is a Dutch merchant called Maximilian [Van der Lever], who, like the rest of his nation, is diligent and industrious to improve the commodities of this kingdom. He makes suit to the Lord Deputy that a colony of Hollanders may be planted on the islands in this lough. If his demands be not unreasonable we [the Commissioners] wish his suit may be granted; for a plantation of the Dutch in this place will be a great encouragement and benefit to the undertakers; for by their industry all the commodities will be wrought and vented [manufactured and exported], and the lake will be so full of boats and barke that they will be a great help to all the civil inhabitants round about." Perhaps, indeed, there was no period in the ancient or medieval history of Ireland, or even in comparatively modern times, during which the North men, or their descendants, under one name or other, were not known either as invaders or traders around the coasts of Ulster, or by the shores of its loughs. We have very early records of their presence at Strangford, Lough Foyle, Lough Erne, Lough Gall, and other such attractive places. An old chronicler has left it on record that "it was impossible for the Irish to free themselves from the brutal and implacable hordes of Norsemen, because of their thirst and their hunger for the fruitful, smooth-plained, and sweet grass lands of Erin, with its fishful rivers and bays." The same instincts brought Maximilian and his friends to Enniskillen in 1609, where, indeed, they appear to have been doing a little trading before that date.

When the Commissioners got to work in Fermanagh, they commenced with the barony of Glancally, or Clancally, now Clonkelly. This barony or plantation precinct is in the extreme eastern part of the county, and contains 30,922 acres. Its northern border consists of upland tracts, but the surface generally is low-lying, and slopes to the south west, forming a part of the east side in the basin system of the Erne. Clonkelly is a comparatively small barony, and contains only part of the two parishes of Clones and Galloon. Its one little village is named Rosslea. The Commissioners only could find in it 5,000 acres of arable land, which they marked off into four proportions—two of the middle size, 1,500 acres each, and two of the small size, 1,000 acres each. These four proportions made five of 1,000 acres each, which were afterwards allotted to five English undertakers, whose names are as follow, viz.:—Sir Hugh Worrall,

Knight; Robert Bogas, Esq.; Robert Calvert, gent.; John Sedborough, Esq.; and Thomas Flowerdew, Esq. When these English planters had been fully twelve months in possession, Sir George Carew reported from Clonkelly as follows:—"Thomas Flowerdew, 2,000 acres; is resident; has cast a trench about an old rath, and is building an English house of 50 feet long and 22 feet broad; providing materials. John Sedborough, 1,000 acres; is resident with his wife and family; has felled timber, raised stones, set up an oven and two chimneys in his house, and intends to go in hand with his bawne. Robert Calvert, 1,000 acres; is resident; has built a house after the English fashion; has two families of English, unto whom he will give estates; six other families have promised to come to him at May next. Robert Bogas, 1,000 acres; has not appeared, nor any for him; nothing done." Of Sir Hugh Worrall it is stated by a scribe named Philip Gatisfeth, "that he [Worrall] hath his brother there taking up his rent, but as yet nothing goes forward."

Not much is known of the five planters above named. 1. Sir Hugh Worrall was a lawyer and had some employments as an agent for the Government. He wanted to undertake for a large proportion of 2,000 acres, but only succeeded in purchasing the small one of 1,000 acres called Ardmagh from Thomas Plumstead. As an apology for his delay in attending to plantation duties, there is the following note to Chichester from the Council in London:—"Sir Hugh Worrall, Knight, undertaker in Ulster, being detained by suits beyond the time prescribed by the proclamation, prays a licence of absence for two months, which we have granted. And, one of his deputies settled there to oversee his proportion being dead, he has appointed one Richard Cotes in his room, under whose charge he intends to send over presently twenty English to inhabit part of his proportion. We accordingly accept the said Cotes as his deputy, so as he send over the said twenty English presently. April 30, 1611." 2. Robert Bogas was one of the forty applicants for the whole County of Fermanagh, as above mentioned. On that list he named his place of residence in England, Densham Park, Suffolk; but in his grant he is styled of Braham in Brantham, Suffolk. He soon sold his proportion of Cloncarn to Edward Hatton, and does not appear to have ever visited it. 3. Robert Calvert's place of residence in England is not known. He settled for a time on his proportion of Gortgunan, and expended a little in improvements, but he soon sold his lands to George Ridgeway, a brother of Sir Thomas Ridgeway, the Treasurer at War. 4. John Sedborough's place of residence in England is not known, but he became an energetic planter. Philip Gatisfeth, above quoted, has mentioned that "Mr. Sudborough has with him eight men well armed, including two sons and one Mr. Stookes, a leaseholder; he has contrived an Irish house into three rooms and built a wattled chimney in it; he has one plough of mares and garrons, an English horse and mare, and twenty head of cows." He died before 1629, and his granddaughter, Barbara, the child of his deceased son, Peter Sedborough, became his heir. She was nineteen years of age at the time of her grandfather's death, and soon afterwards married John Mayne. In 1630, the lands of Gortgunan were sold to Lord Robert Dillon and Francis Annesley, who had been created Lord Mountnorris. 5. Thomas Flowerdew was one of the forty applicants for the whole County of Fermanagh, and on that list it was stated that he had come from Hetherset, in the County of Norfolk. Philip Gatisfeth, perhaps an assistant of Sir George Carew, stated that "Thomas Flowerdew has built an Irish house with a chimney at the end made of wattles, contrived into two rooms, and a frame for a timber house of birch, most part to be set up in a Dane's Fort." He died before 1629, as in that year there was a regrant in his proportion called Lisresk to his son Edward Flowerdew.

From the barony of Clonkelly the Commissioners passed into a precinct made up of the half-baronies of Lurghe and Coolmakernan, and now comprised in the barony of Lurg. This barony lies in the extreme north of the county, and contains 82,939 acres, including Boa Island, and at least two thirds of all the islands in lower Lough Erne. It contains the whole of the parishes of Beleek, Drumkerran, and Magheraculmoney, with part of the parishes of Derryvullane, Magheracross, Templecarne, and Trory; its towns and chief villages are Beleek, Lisnarrick, Lowtherstown, Ederney, Kesh, Leck, and part of Pettigoe. In this precinct the Commissioners only found 9,000 acres arable, which they marked off into eight proportions—two of 1,500 acres each, and six of 1,000 acres each. These proportions were soon afterwards distributed amongst seven English planters or undertakers, named respectively Thomas Flowerdew, Esq.; Thomas Blenerhassett, Esq.; Sir Edward Blenerhassett, Knight; John Archdale, Esq.; Edward Warde, gentleman; Thomas Barton, Esq.; Henry Honynge or Hunning, Esq. Respecting three of these planters, Carew reports, after twelve months' occupancy, as follows:—"Edward Warde, 1,000 acres; has not appeared, nor any one for him; nothing done. Henry Honynge or Hunning, 1,000 acres; has taken possession, but nothing done. John Archdale, 1,000 acres; nothing done." 1. Thomas Blenerhassett came from Horseford, in the County of Norfolk. He held a middle proportion called Edernagh, and named his residence therein Castlehassett. He left two sons. 2 Sir Edward Blenerhassett is supposed to have been a brother of Thomas, as their lands lay side by side on the shore of Lough Erne. Sir Edward left a son named Francis, who resided on his lands,

Banahmore, in Fermanagh. 3. John Archdale came from Darsham, in the County of Suffolk. He died before 1629, as in that year his son Edward Archdale had a regrant of his estate. 4. Edward Warde came from the County of Suffolk, and in 1611 sold his proportion of Nakarney to Harrington Sutton, of Kallam, in the County of Nottingham. The latter soon afterwards disposed of it to Sir Gerrard Lowther, whose father conducted Mary Queen of Scots to the Castle of Carlisle on her arrival in England. This Sir Gerrard Lowther was appointed Lord Chancellor in 1654. He sold his lands in Fermanagh before 1630, as in that year they were granted to Sir William Parsons and Sir Adam Loftus. The latter was the founder of the family of Ely. 5. John Barton came from Norwich, and sold his proportion of Dromunshyn to Sir Gerrard Lowther and Henry Flowerdew. 6. Henry Honynge came from Darsham, in Suffolk, but he appears to have made no attempt to plant his proportion of Dowrosse, although the lands were afterwards known as the Manor of Runingstown.

III.

Thomas Blenerhasset, previously named, wrote a tract about the "Ulster Plantation," and addressed it to the "Mighty and High-renowned Prince Henry"—eldest son of James I. In this production the author recommends the institution or appointment of a great periodical hunt in Ulster for the destruction alike of wolves and woodkerne, together with all such of the inhabitants as could be found to sympathise with or shelter the latter! Here are his words:—"When the spaces in the woods be cut out, and the bogges be made somewhat passible, then these new erected townes intending a reformation must oftentimes at the first set a universal great hunt, that a suddane search may be made in all suspitious places, for the woolfe and the woodkerne, which, being secretly and wisely appointed by the governors, they, with the help of some Irish, well acquainted with the holes and holdes of those offenders, the generalitie [the rank and file] shall search every particular place. For an example, the fourth day of March, the Lyfford, the Omagh, they in Fermanagh, Donganon, and Colrayne shall, on that day, send forth from every one of those places an hundred men; which five hundred men shall then make search in all the most suspitious places; and by being at one instant dispersed with furniture [weapons] fit for such business, they shall discover all the caves, holes, and lurking places of that country, even for an hundred miles compasse; and no doubt it will be a pleasant hunt, and much prey will fall to the followers, for what doth escape some will fall into the hands of others, and bring such a terror that the woolfe himself will not dare to continue his haunt where such so suddane incursions shall be used, although it be but once in a month, the charge none, the pleasure much, the profit more. Then may they make enclosures and venture their cattle abroad—for to starve in the night doth overthrow the feed in the day—with the general improvement and chief profit, for the feeding of all kinds of cattle. Then may they sow, mow, plant, and thrive and be merry, for this kind of planting will not only supplant those domestic animals, but there will be out of those townes five thousand well armed men to encounter any foreign enemy that shall offer arrival to invade, whereby his Majesty shall shortly have little need of those chargeable garrisons; for these undertakers will easily restrain the mutinies of them at home, and confront the power of any invader whatsoever; and those good fellows in trowzes — I mean the everywhere dispersed creatures in the create—seeing this course, will no longer hearken after change, nor intertain the lurking woodkerne, as they now do." The periodical hunt was not appointed in exactly the form here recommended, but it was practically and remorselessly carried out at convenient times and on fitting occasions throughout the six plantation counties, under the superintendence of the several provost-marshalls.

The Commissioners on leaving Lurg passed on to the barony of Knockninney which extends from the head to nearly the foot of upper Lough Erne, and includes about a third of that upper lake and its islands. The surface of this barony may be described, indeed, as an expanse of lakes, swamps, meadows, and low lying fields, varied by patches of arable lands and bogs. It comprises 30,604 acres, and contains part of the parishes of Kinawley, Tomregan, and Galloon. In this barony, or plantation precinct, the Commissioners found 9,000 acres of arable land which was marked off into six proportions—two of each of the three sizes. These proportions were allotted afterwards to six Scottish undertakers, whose names were as follow—viz., Michael Balfour, Lord Burley; Michael Balfour, jun., Laird Mountwhany; Sir John Wischart, Knight, Laird Pettaro; Thomas Moneypenny, Laird of Kinkell; James Trayle, Esq.; and George Smellhome, gent.—1. Michael Balfour, Lord Burley, was the eldest son of Sir James Balfour of Pittendreich and Mountwhany, in Fifeshire. He got two proportions in Knockninney—viz., the large proportion of Legan, 2,000 acres; and the small proportion of Carrowshee, 1,000 acres. He left two sons and a daughter; his second son, James Balfour, was created Lord Glenawley, and succeeded to his father's property in Fermanagh. His daughter married a Scotch husband named Arnot, so wealthy that he paid all his wife's family debts, and, taking the name of Balfour, obtained also the title of Lord Burley. 2 Michael Balfour, jun., was the elder son of old Lord Burley, and was known as Laird of Mountwhany. He got the middle-sized proportion of Kilspinan, but sold it soon to Sir Stephen Butler, and it now forms part of the estate of the Earl of Erne. 3. Sir John Wishart was the son of an Earl of Angus, a great landowner in the Mearns. His quarrels with James Spottiswoode, Bishop of Clogher, were notorious in Fermanagh. The Bishop spoke of him as "one Sir John Wishard, sometime Lord Pittaro in Scotland, who, having consumed his estate there, begged some escheated lands in the Counsy of Fermanagh." Wischart sold his middle proportion of Leitrim to Stephen Butler. The latter built his house on the site of the old Castle of the O'Cassidy's, the hereditary physicians of the Maguires. The same site is now occupied by the magnificent residence of the Earl of Belmore, and is still known by the old name of Castlecoole. 4. Thomas Moneypenny was also a Fifeshire Laird, but the lands of Kinkell, near St. Andrews, know his curious surname no more. He sold his proportion of Aghalane to Thomas Crichton, ancestor of the Earls of Erne. Although Moneypenny sold out his estate in Fermanagh, he probably settled in Ulster as persons of his name appeared prominently during the insurrection of 1641, and afterwards. 5. James Trayle came probably from Fifeshire also. He sold his proportion of Dresternan in 1615 to George Adwick, who soon afterwards sold it to Sir Stephen Butler. Trayle settled in Ulster, although parting with his original estate in Fermanagh. His descendants now write their surname Traill, not Trayle. 6 George Smelholme came from Leith. He sold his proportion called Dirriany to Sir Stephen Butler, and returned to Scotland.

From Knockniany the Commissioners went to the barony of Magheriboy, which is still so-called, and which lies in the north-west of the county. It contains 94,171 acres, and includes the whole of the parish of Devenish, and part of the parishes of Bohoe, Cleemish, Enniskillen, Inismacsaint, Rossory, and Trory. It contains part of the town of Enniskillen, and the villages of Churchhill and Derrygonnelly. The Commissioners here also found 9,000 arable acres, which they marked off into six proportions — two of each of the three sizes. These proportions were afterwards allotted to seven Scottish undertakers whose names were Sir John Home, or Hume, Knight; Robert Hamilton, Esq; James Gibb, gent.; Jerome Lindsey, Esq; William Fowler, Esq.; Alexander Home, or Hume, Esq.; and John Dunbarr, Esq. Carew reported of the planters in Magheriboy, after the first twelve months of their plantation life, as follows:—"Sir John Home, Knight, 2,000 acres; has taken possession, returned to Scotland; nothing done, or any agent present. Robert Hamilton, 1,500 acres; has been here to see the land, but has not taken possession, and nothing done. But since our return [to Dublin from Ulster] he is arrived in Fermanagh, as we are informed, with 18 tenants and artificers for planting; with 60 head of cattle, 10 horses and mares for labour; is felling timber, and providing materials for building. William Fowler, 1,500 acres; taken possession, returned into Scotland; nothing done. James Gibb, 1,000 acres, the like. Jerome Lindsey, 1,000 acres; took possession by attorney; did nothing else. Alexander Home, 1,000 acres; the like. John Dunbarr, 1,000 acres; has taken possession, returned into Scotland, and sent over six persons, whereof two are freeholders, one a tenant for years, and two tenants at will; some building in hand; 8 horses for work brought over, with money to provide materials. Mr. Hamilton has come lately, and with him 10 people, with 14 garrons and horses, and is buying cattle daily; is about to set up a plough or two instantly; as yet nothing built. Mr. Dunbarr's brother is there taking up his duties and rent, but doth nothing else that I see. For all the rest, some of them came and saw the land, and went their ways, but what order they took I know not, and what is above written is all that I have seen." Gatisfeth, whoever he may have been, has the following note:—"Sir John Hume's man is there receiving his rent and duties, but nothing done."

Thus, it would appear that the planters in Magheriboy, as in nearly all the other baronies, had done little or nothing during the first year. 1. Sir John Hume was a son of Alexander Hume, of Manderstown, in Berwickshire, and brother of the well-known George Hume, created Earl of Dunbar. Sir John, who came to Fermanagh, selected one of the most beautiful sites for his residence on all that charming Lough Erne. This residence, known as Tully Castle, stood on the high point of the shore north-west of Inismacsaint—Inismuighesamh, "the island of the sorrel plain," and the views from the ivy clad ruins are specially attractive. At this point on its western shore, Lough Erne spreads out its greatest expanse of water, presenting to the eye a bewildering number of beautifully wooded islands. Tully Castle was burned in 1641, and never rebuilt, and Hume Castle from that date became the family residence. The name of Sir John Hume's proportion was Ardgort, the high field. 2. Robert Hamilton was a relative of James Hamilton, Lord Clandeboy, and in the time of Pynnar's survey, 1618-20, he was styled Sir Robert Hamilton. He sold his proportion, called Derrynafogher, in 1614, to Archibald Hamilton, and from him they passed to his son, Malcolm Hamilton, Chancellor of Down, and afterwards Archbishop of Cashel. 3. James Gibb was the son of John Gibb, a Scottish servant in the King's household. He sold his proportion, called Dromra, to James Hamilton, of Keckton, and the latter sold it to John Archdale. 4. Jerome Lindsey was also a King's servant, and had originally come from Leith. In 1612 he sold his proportion, called Drumskeagh, to Sir William Cole. 5. William Fowler was another servant of the King, but specially employed by the Queen. In October, 1608, there is a note from the Earl of Shrewsbury to Salisbury, greatly recommending Fowler to his notice as a person well qualified for the Queen's service. In 1615 Fowler sold his proportion of Moyglasse to Sir John Hume. 6. Alexander Hume was a younger brother of Sir John, to whom he sold his proportion of Drumcoose, returning in 1626 to the family residence of Manderstown, in the parish of Dunse, Berwickshire. Sir John Hume had thus, from time to time, become the owner of extensive estates in Fermanagh, which were inherited by his son, Sir George Hume. In 1736 Nicholas Loftus, the first Earl of Ely, married Mary Hume, and their son, the second Earl of Ely, inherited the united estates of his father and mother. The two family mansions of Castle Hume and Ely Lodge stand opposite to each other on the eastern and western shores of Lough Erne. 7. John Dunbarr was the grandson of Sir John Dunbar, of Mocrum, whose property now forms a part of the Earl of Galloway's estate on the northern and eastern shores of Garlieston Bay. This undertaker did not come to settle permanently in Fermanagh until 1615, although he secured legal possession of his proportion called Drumcro in 1610. He was descended from an Earl of Dunbar, who married a daughter of Robert Bruce, and he brought with him to Fermanagh a sword which had belonged to Bruce—a family relic which had been piously preserved at Mocrum during many generations. John Dunbarr's granddaughter was married to Hugh Montgomery, of Derrygonelly, near Enniskillen, and with her the sword came to her husband's house. The writer of the Montgomery Manuscripts, after being on a visit to his kinsman, Hugh Montgomery, of Derrygonelly, refers to this sword thus—"I saw a rarity at that house, to wit, a two-edged sword of excellent metal, which this Hugh never ceased to be made, but had it in the late war about Enniskillen. I am of the opinion there is no smith in Ireland could forge so good a blade, for I saw it severely tried. The sword is inscribed on the right-hand side of the blade thus :—

"Robertus Bruscius,
Scotorum Rex, 1310 ;"

and on the reverse side

"Pro Christo et Patria."

There are some obliterated or worn out words supposed to be the cutler's name, the letters being but by halves and quarters, whereof we could make nothing." Where may this sword be now ? Probably among the contents of some lumber-room in Fermanagh. Surely it must have been preserved by the descendants of Hugh Montgomery, of Derrygonelly.

From Magheriboy the Commissioners took their way to the precinct of Clinawley, now known as the barony of Glenawley, which lies along the west side of Fermanagh, and contains 75,469 acres. It contains the whole of the parish of Kelleeher, and part of the parishes of Bohoe, Cleenish, Kinawley, and Rossory. [In this barony the Commissioners only found 6,000 acres arable, which they marked off into four proportions — two great and two small. These proportions were subsequently allotted to three servitors, a portion of the barony being also set apart for such natives in the County Fermangh as had got small grants. The names of the three servitors were Sir John Davys, Knight ; Samuel Harrison, Esq. ; and Peter Moistin or Mostyn, gent. 1. Sir John Davys, the Attorney-General, had, no doubt, selected his position in this precinct when visiting the neighbourhood as a commissioner. The lands in his proportion, called Derricurra, included those of Lisgoole Abbey, and extended thence to the vicinity of Enniskillen. They occupied the very centre of that sylvan, meadowy, and wheat-bearing district. He had other lands in other counties of Ulster, but this estate in Fermanagh appears to have been to himself more interesting than the others. When rules were being drawn up to regulate the choice of such servitors as were to be undertakers, one rule was laid down that no servitors but "martial" men were to be admitted, saving Mr. Attorney General, who may have a middle proportion in Clinawley, near Lisgoole. 2. Samuel Harrison. 3. Peter Moystin. Nothing was specially known as to the birthplaces or families of these two servitors. When Pynnar visited the district, 1618-20, he reported that Harrison was dead, and his widow had done nothing in building on her 500 acres. Moyston's portion of 300 acres had no buildings, and the owner of them was living in Connaught.

IV.

From Clinawley, or Glenawley, the Commissioners passed into the only remaining precinct in Fermanagh, which they designated the precinct of Coole and Tircannada, and which now comprises the two present baronies of Coole and Tyrkennedy. The barony of Coole contains only about 21,000 acres, and is situate in the south-east corner of the county. It is divided into two nearly equal parts by the road from Cavan to Enniskillen running through Newtownbutler. The central parts of Coole are comparatively rough and boggy, but the districts along the margin of Lough Erne, and those including the Castle Sanderson and Belmont demesnes, are fertile and well wooded. This barony of Coole contains part of the parishes of Currin, Drummully, and Galloon; but it has only one town, Newtownbutler, which from its position is very much admired.

The barony of Tyrkennedy lies on the eastern or right hand side of the lough, and contains 54,685 acres, its water area comprising a considerable portion of Upper Lough Erne, and also of that connecting link between the two lakes. This barony contains part of the parishes of Cleenish, Derrybrusk, Derryvullane, Enniskillen, Magheracross, and Trory. The only town is part of Enniskillen, and the chief villages are Lisbellaw, Tempo, and Ballinamallard. The Commissioners here found 10,000 acres of arable land, which they marked off into ten proportions of 1,000 acres each. These ten proportions were afterwards allotted to four servitors and two natives of high rank, other portions of the barony being granted in small parcels to native gentry in the county.

The names of the four servitors were Sir Henry Folliott, Knight; Roger Atkinson, gent.; William Cole, Esq.; and Paul Gore, Esq. The names of the two natives were Bryan Maguire and Con Mac Shane O'Neill. 1. Sir Henry Folliott had grants of extensive lands in Donegal prior to the plantation. His lands in Fermanagh were known as the manor of Drumshine. He was created Baron Folliott, of Ballyshannon, in 1619. The title became extinct at the death of his grandson, the third Lord Folliott, in 1716. 2. Roger Atkinson came to Ireland as a servitor in 1596, and after the close of the seven years' war he got a pension of four shillings a day, probably as a spy. In 1604 he was appointed provost-marshal of Lough Foyle, and of the forces and garrisons in the City of Derry, or elsewhere in Ulster. 3. William Cole was warmly recommended by the Council in London to Chichester in 1610. "The Council are satisfied of Captain William Cole's sufficiency to maintain a reasonable proportion, and are aware of his merits. As he has a commission for the charge of his Majesty's boats in Lough Yearne, and for the keeping of the Castle Enniskillen, the Council suggest that he should be assigned a servitor's proportion as near as may be to the said castle, which, otherwise, will be very destitute of demesne, as the lands next adjacent to the castle have fallen to the lot of some Scottish gentleman, and cannot be altered." It is hardly necessary to say that this suggestion from the supreme authority was carefully followed out by the Deputy, and that Cole forthwith was put into the possession of suitable lands known afterwards as the manor of Corrigrade. Carew's account of Enniskillen in 1611 is as follows :—"There is a fair strong wall newly erected, of lime and stone, twenty six foot high, with flankers and a parapet, and a walk on the top of the wall, built by Captain William Colle, constable thereof, towards which he had £200 sterling from the King. A fair house begun upon the foundation of the old castle, with other convenient houses for store and munition, which, besides laying out the captain's own money, will draw on some increase of charge to the King. The bawne is ditched about with a fair large ditch and a river on one side, with a good drawbridge. The King has three good boats there ready to attend all services. A large piece of ground adjoins the fort, with a good timber house, after the English fashion, built by the captain, in which he and his family now dwell." 4. Paul Gore was the eldest son of Gerrard Gore, a merchant tailor and alderman of London. He came to Ireland in command of a troop of horse, just after the defeat of the English by the Earl of Tyrone, at the Yellow Ford, on the Blackwater, in the year 1598. Gore's proportion in Fermanagh, called Carrick, included the island of Ballymacmanus, in Lough Erne, now known as Ballisle, and once the residence of Cathal Maguire, who there compiled the very valuable fragment of Irish history known as the "Annals of Ulster." Captain Paul Gore left two sons, named Ralph and Arthur. Ralph, who succeeded, was ancestor of the Earls of Ross. Arthur settled at Newtowngore, in the County of Mayo, and married a daughter of Sir George St. George, of Carrick, in the County of Leitrim. His grandson, also named Arthur, was advanced to the peerage as Baron Saunders, of Deeps, in the County of Wexford, and Viscount Sudley, of Castle-Gore, in the County of Mayo. In 1759 he was created Earl of Arran—deriving the name of his Earldom from the County of Galway. The two chief residences of the Earls of Arran were Newtongore, in Mayo, and Saunders-Court, in Wexford.

The only members of the old main family of the Maguires who got portions of their own lands were Bryan and Tirlagh, two younger brothers of Sir Hugh and Cuconaght already mentioned. Sir George Carew stated in 1611 that Brian and Tirlagh had removed to their proportions assigned to them in the precinct of Coole and Tyrcannada, where they had built a great coppled house, in which they dwelt, although Tirlagh did not live long after his removal. The name of their manor was Inseyloughgeasse, and their lands there contained 2,500 acres. In Pynnar's time, 1618 20, Bryan had made progress. His manor was then called Tempodessell (now Tempo), and he had built a good house of lime and stone, but he and all his tenants continued the old Irish custom of ploughing their horses by the tail. Bryan left one son named Hugh, who married a lady of the principal family of the O'Reillys, and by her left a son named Cuconaght Mor Maguire. The last named married a daughter of Heber Maginis, of Castlewellan. He mortgaged a large portion of his estate to raise and support a regiment of horse in the service of James II., and was slain fighting gallantly at the battle of Aughrim. On the day after the battle one of his followers cut off his head and carried it reverently to the island of Devenish, where he interred it in the family tomb of the Maguires. Cuconaght Mor's great grandson, Hugh Maguire, of Tempo, is described as one of the finest men, both in bodily proportion and mental power, in the long line of his Clann-Colla ancestors. He had to part, however, with the remainder of the family estate, and his sons were eventually obliged to work as common sailors—another illustration of the truth of Dean Swift's statement, that the representatives of the old Irish nobility were to be found, after the plantations, amongst the humblest inhabitants of the land. The Tempo estate is now owned, we believe, by a son of the late Sir James Emerson Tennent.

The continuance of the barbarous practice of ploughing by the tail was greatly owing to the discreditable conduct of the Government. The following extract from a report by Commissioners appointed to investigate the matter is instructive :—"The barbarous use of Ploughing with Garrons tyed by the Tails was restrained by the Council here [in Ireland]. Afterwards the same was permitted, and a mulct imposed of 10s for every short plough, which forfeiture, in Anno 1612, was granted to Sir William Udale, whose patent is still in force. And where it was directed that the Patentee should be compounded with, and the same taken into your Majesty's owne hands, we find nothing done in that kinde ; but by a letter from the Lords of the Councell in England, your Majesty requires the Deputy to give warrant to the Patentee to levy the penalties as before ; by which meanes this barbarous custome of ploughing with horses tyed by the tailes is still continued in many places, for restraint whereof we finde no law or statute here in force. And the countrie hath renewed their complaints that this annual execution of 10s for every short plough hath, in many places, impoverished the countrie ; and, by colour thereof, from some have been taken and extorted money for their harrowes, as we are informed ; and of some of less ability composition made at less rates than the penaltie of 10s appointed, as was directlie proved ; so that the use of this patent leads more to a private gaine than to a Reformacion; in regard whereof, and the due consideration of the now scarcity of corne, and the povertie of this people, we conceive it fitt that short ploughs should be tollerated till the first of Aprile and no longer; that in the meantime men may furnish themselves with such ploughs as are in use in England, or learn to use their short ploughs, setting their garrons three or four horses affront, which is free from unseemliness and fitter for some mountainous and boggish grounds than the long plough, as is now begun and practised in the barony of Clankie [Clonkee], in the Countie of Cavan, which we rather advise, because we have received credible informacion that the Earle of Antrim, in the Countie of Antrim, where he hath divers baronies, hath banished that barbarous custome by holdinge all the tenants to the fashion of English ploughing; and Sir George Hamilton hath already reformed his tenants, and so others. And your Majesty's aime appearinge by all the Acts to tend reformacion of the abuse, and to remove the barbarous practice, we offer to your Majesty's consideracion whether it were not fitt that a Proclamation bee published, inhibiting all your subjects hereafter the first day of Aprile next, from plowing with garrons or bullock tyed by the tailes upon pain of your high displeasure, and such as shall offend to be bounde to their good behaviours till they reforme." It is remarkable with what tenacity the Irish, in some districts, clung to this method of ploughing—and under the impression, too, that it was more humane than the English method! It appears, however, that the real object of the several orders in Council against the practice was not to abolish it, but to raise money on fines for permission to continue it. Sir Charles Cornwallis, writing in October, 1621, to Lord Northampton on the subject of an earlier commission, says—"Your Lordship will understand by their labours what great sums of money have been drawn out of the supposed commisseration of the hinder parts of these poor Irish garrons."

Only forty-five natives in the County Fermanagh got small grants in the baronies of Glenawley and Tyrkennedy. Several of these represented noble Irish families, and the others belonged to the rank of gentry, being styled "gentlemen" in their several grants from the Crown. The great majority of them were Maguires, with a sprinkling of MacHughes, O'Corcorans, Mulronys, and O'Flanaghans.

In Blenerhasset's Tract on the Ulster plantation, which has been already quoted, the author strenuously urged all Englishmen who wished to better their worldly circumstances, or increase their sources of enjoyment, to come to Ulster without delay. His rhapsodies, although contemptible, are somewhat curious, as exhibiting the tone and style of expression by which the undertakers generally sought to make known their aims in Ulster, and especially to recommend the whole movement as affording a splendid opportunity for the accumulation of wealth to those who zealously embarked therein. "Art thou a tradesman," he exclaims, "a smith, a weaver, a mason, or a carpenter? Go thither, thou shalt be there in estimation, and quickly enriched by thy endeavours. Art thou a husbandman whose worth is not past ten or twenty pounds? Go thither, those new manormakers [undertakers] will make thee a copyholder; thou shalt whistle sweetly, and feed thy whole family, if they be six, for sixpence the day. Art thou a gentleman that takest pleasure in the hunt? The fox, the woolfe, and woodkerne do expect thy coming; and the comely, well cabbased [well-fed] stag will furnish thy feast with a full dish; there thou shalt have elbow-room, the eagle and the earne, and all sorts of high-flying fowls do attend thee. Art thou a minister of God's Word? Make speed, the harvest is great, but the labourers be few; thou shalt there see the poor, ignorant, untaught people worship stones and sticks; thou, by carrying millions to heaven, mayest be made an archangel, and have, whilst thou dost live, of worldly respects what not. So Ulster, which hath been hitherto the receptacle and very den of rebels and devouring creatures, shall far excel Munster, and the civilest part of all that country; and peradventure in civility and sincere religion equal even fair England herself, with a Christian and comfortable society of neighbourhood; and so they, at least 300,000 souls, besides children [in all Ireland—but what of the millions to be carried by the ministers to heaven ?], may come unto the true knowledge of God, and by faith in Jesus Christ may be made free from everlasting damnation. So the King's Majesty shall be disburdened of a very great charge out of the Exchequer, the country safely secured unto the Crown, and we his Majesty's subjects enriched by our endeavours, which God of His unspeakable mercy grant, for His dear Son Jesus Christ, His sake. Amen. Fair England, thy flourishing sister, brave Hibernia, commendeth unto thy due consideration her youngest daughter, depopulated Ulster, not doubting how the long continuance of lamentable wars have razed and utterly defaced whatsoever was beautiful in her to behold, and has so bereaved all her royalties, goodly ornaments, and well-beseeming tyres, as that there remaineth but only the majesty of her naked personage, which even in that plight is such as whosoever shall seek and search all Europe's best bowers shall not find many that may make with her comparison! Behold the admirable worth of her worthiness! Even now she gives the world to understand, by testimonial known unto all men that know her, that if thou wilt now but assist her with means to erect her ruins, she will nourish thee with much dainty provision, and so furnish thee, as thou shalt not need to send to thy neighbour kingdoms for corn, nor to the Netherlands for fine Holland; she will, in requital for thy kindness, provide those things, with some others such as thy heart most desireth. Art thou over-charged with much people? Ulster will embrace that, thy overplus, in her amorous, sweet arms; she will place them, as it were, by Euphrates, and feed them with better ambrosia than ever Jupiter himself knew."

We have next concluding references to affairs in Fermanagh and Londonderry in the following terms:—"The County of Fermanagh, MackGueres country, rejoice; many undertakers, all incorporated in mind as one, with their followers there, seek and desire to settle themselves. Woe to the woolfe and the wood-kerne! The islands in Lougheарne shall have habitations, a fortified corporation, market towns, and many new erected manors shall now so beautify her desolation that her inaccessible woods, with spaces tractable, shall no longer nourish devourers, but, by the sweet society of loving neighbourhood, shall entertain humanity even in the best fashion. Go on, worthy gentlemen, fear not; the God of Heaven will assist and protect you, the rather for that simply of yourselves you do desire to perform so honourable an action. And they, the successors of high-renowned Lud, will there re-edify a new Troy. Their [the London Corporation's] spacious coffers have the receipts of England's treasures; and the continual resplendency of his Majesty's presence does so illustrate their super-exceeding good, that all, whatsoever by may be thought of, or by policy of man devised, so much absolutely have they [the Londoners] from thence, therefore they will not capitulate [surrender] the fresh and flourishing County of Coleraine, with the exceeding beauty of the Band [Bann]. They have O'Kanes country, and whatsoever Ireland's Eden can afford, and therefore, even in respect of their own reputation, they of themselves will perform this the most honourable action that ever they attempted. [At first the Londoners dreaded the release and return of O'Cahan to his estates, until he was sent from Dublin to the Tower in London] Therefore, let Coleraine rejoice, for the heart of England, London herself, will, no doubt, make her more beautiful than many, and furnish Loughfoyle with a goodly fleet. O powerful England, if thou wilt extend thy bounty to others less able to perform such designs, then they also will undertake the other counties, so as within three years their endeavours shall bring thee and thine altogether out of doubt, ever hereafter to be charged with any taxation for her [Ulster's] defence; for certainly she shall shortly be able rather to lend than to borrow aid. Let not, then, these kind undertakers want any kind of kindness. Little do many of thy [England's] inhabitants care to spend a pound or two at a merry meeting, and presently it is forgotten. Let every man of worth give but his crown to this honourable intention and merry meeting, and it shall remain as a crown of glory to everlasting posterity, and free every one of them peradventure from the expense of many pounds. And this trophy, of all thy triumphs the most renowned, obtained with the lives of many thousands of thy soldiers—as everywhere dispersed . skulls of slain men do there at this present manifestly declare—if it be now neglected, thy next neighbours, and those of thy princes and people far remote, will suppose thee very poor both in power and policy. And thus, fair England, having laid before thy amiable eyes how Ulster, now naked, may be decked and richly adorned, and thyself certainly disburdened of much: I refer the effecting thereof to the King's most excellent Majesty, who hath power to command, and will no doubt provide for Ulster's prosperity."

THE COUNTY OF CAVAN.

I.

In former times the whole region now comprising the counties of Cavan and Leitrim constituted one great territory, and was known as Breifne, or Brennie. It was occupied by two powerful but distinct tribes or clans — the O'Reillys and O'Rourkes. The eastern section, now Cavan, was held by the O'Reillys, and was known as Brennie O'Reilly; whilst the western portion, being the country of the O'Rourkes, was known as Brennie O'Rourke. The O'Reillys, anciently the O'Raghallaigh, descended from an early Ulster chieftain of the O'Neills, and were popularly designated as "of the red arms" and as "of the rough incursions," because of their fierce methods of warfare. East Breifne, or Cavan, originally belonged to the province of Connaught, but so soon as the English were able to establish their government north of the Pale, they found that Cavan could be more effectively managed if annexed to Ulster. When the Lord Deputy Sussex, in 1562, reported to the Council in London on the state of Connaught, he referred to East Breifne as follows:—"O'Raillie's country is taken to be within Connaught, but because it lieth fitter for another government [Ulster], and bordereth upon the English Pale, I leave it out of the government of Connaught." And left out of the western province Cavan thenceforth was, being considered ever since as one of the counties of Ulster. It contains 301,000 Irish acres, or 433,573 acres English measure. It is now divided into eight baronies, viz.:—Tullaghagh, in the north-west; Lower Loughtee, in the north; Tullaghgarvey, in the north-east; Clonkee, in the east; Castlerahen, in the south-east; Clonmahon, in the south;

Tullyhunco, in the west; and Upper Loughtee, in the centre.

In 1606 Chichester sent the following account of affairs in Cavan to the Council:—"The Cavan is a spacious and large county, very populous, and the people hardy and warlike. The chief of them are the O'Realyes, of which surname there are several septs, most of them cross and opposite one to another. By the division and separation among themselves, the whole county, which heretofore made their dependency upon the chief of the sept, may, with the more facility and assurance, be divided into parcels, and disposed to several freeholders, who, depending immediately upon the King, will not fear or obey their neighbours [their former legitimate chiefs or headmen] unless some one or two be made so powerful as to overtop and sway down the rest; and therefore care must be taken in the settlement of this country that the greatest part of the people have their dependency immediately on the King, and as little on the Irish Lords as may be without apparent hindrance to the plantation and settlement of the country. We must note that there are many freeholders as they pretend who will expect a good portion of the barony of Loughtee, besides that which is intended for the town, the Castle of Cloughouter, and Belturbet; whereby it may be conceived that the head of the house will be left in a meaner state than one of the inferior freeholders, if other care be not taken for him; and therefore a consideration must be had upon the division how he may be relieved by allotting some portions of land unto him, out of the other baronies, or by reserving unto him some chief rents from the freeholders, the rather because his father was slain in the late Queen's service, and because he was descended by the mother from the house of Ormonde."

The "head of the house,' the then representative chief of the O'Reillys, about whom Chichester thus appears to have had a little becoming anxiety, was young Mulmorie or Myles O'Reilly, whose father had fallen at the battle of the Yellow Ford, on the Blackwater, fighting for the Government, and whose grandfather, Sir John O'Reilly, had surrendered his claims as territorial chieftain, on condition that he and his heirs were to hold four baronies of the county. But Chichester's scruples soon vanished before the requirements of the coming plantation, and he discovered a much more congenial method of arrangement than this condition implied. "In this county," he explains, "there is a poor town bearing the name of Cavan, seated betwixt many small hills, but the barony in which it stands is named Loughtee, and the best in the countie, being one of the four designed to Sir John O'Realley, and the fittest to be reserved in his Majesty's sole disposition for bringing it to a civil county." In his "Notes of Remembrances" Chichester thus further expatiates on the purposes to which the lands of Loughtee—the best barony in the county—ought to be applied :—"The principal to be cared for is the town of Cavan, which ought to be made a corporation, and about a thousand acres of land laid unto it out of the barony of Loughtee. The castle there to be likewise reserved to the King, and the like allotment of land to be made for the maintenance thereof, and the same to be passed or given to some honest, trusty, and powerful man who shall be able with some small help from the King to rebuild the castle and to stock and manure the land, whose residence there will greatly avail the settlement of that country. Belturbet is likewise by situation a fit place to be strengthened with a ward or other residence of civil people and well affected subjects, by reason it lies on the head of Lough Earne. It has now but a small portion of land belonging to it, and therefore some more should be annexed thereunto and disposed upon some honest and well-affected man as aforesaid, who, for a time, must be enabled by a ward or other help from his Majesty to manure and plant the same. Cloughouter also is a place to be reserved and regarded for. From thence there is a passage by water to Belturbet, and from Belturbet to Belecke, near Ballyshannon; and therefore a like portion of land to be reserved as that of Belturbet. The rest of the barony [of Loughtee] may be disposed in demesne, the chiefry to young Mulmorie O'Relye, the grandchild of Sir John O'Relye."

When the Commissioners of Plantation, however, soon afterwards got to work in the County of Cavan nothing more was heard even of this small chiefry for the youthful and helpless Myles O'Reilly, and eventually he had to rest and be thankful for a "proportion" of the confiscated lands on the same conditions imposed on all other undertakers—even "although his mother was from the house of Ormonde." The Commissioners appointed to mark off the several proportions commenced here with the barony or precinct of Loughtee, wherein they found the scenery very beautiful owing to its proximity to Lough Erne. As Davys had a special eye for the beautiful in nature he got a proportion here also in the choicest soil, but as he had a special eye also to business, he sold his share of the spoil in Loughtee, even before he had the trouble or delay of getting out his patent. The arable lands in this barony were only found to amount to 12,500 acres, although it contains 96,000 statute acres, and is divided into Upper and Lower Loughtee. The upper portion includes part of the present parishes of Crosserlough, Denn, Killinkere, Kilmore, Laragh, and Urney, with the whole of the parishes of Annagcliff, Castleterra, and Lavey. Its towns and villages are Cavan, Ballyhaise, Butler's Bridge, and Stradone. Lower Loughtee is bisected from end to end by the River Erne—from the foot of Loughouter to the head of Upper Lough Erne. It contains part of the parishes of Annagh,

Tomregan, and Urney, with the whole parish of Drumlane. The 12,500 arable acres of this vast territory were marked off into eleven proportions and distributed amongst six undertakers. What remained consisted of church lands, a grant for a school, and a grant for a corporate town. With these exceptions the whole vast residue was thrown in gratuitously to the several "proportions" as unprofitable lands, so that the planters had here also ample room for expansion.

The names of these fortunate planters were Sir Richard Waldron, Knight; John Fishe, Esq.; Sir Stephen Butler, Knight; Sir Hugh Wyrrall, Knight; Sir Nicholas Lusher, Knight; John Tailor, gent.; and William Snow, gent. Carew reported progress here also at the end of their first year of occupancy:—"Sir John Davys, Knight, 2,000 acres, made over his proportion to Mr. Richard Waldron, who passed the same to Mr. Rignold Horne, who sold his estate to Sir Nicholas Lusher, knight; nothing done. John Fishe, 2,000 acres; came over in the summer, took possession, went back again and left his deputy here, and returned with his wife and family about May last [1611]; brought with him artificers and servants of all sorts, thirty-three, or thereabout; two English teams of horses, with English carts, continually employed drawing materials; oaks felled, and carpenters employed in the woods of Fermanagh, felling more; arms of all sorts for thirty-five men; a barrel of powder, with match and lead proportionable. Sir Hugh Wyrrall, or Worral, knight, 1,500 acres; was here in the summer, took possession and returned into England; lady and family came over about the 20th July last. Twenty artificers and servants resident, most of whom lived there all last winter, has built a faire house at Bealturberte, after the English manner, and dwelling houses with a smith's forge. Between Sir Hugh Worral and Mr. Stephan Butler were built, at Bealturberte, five boats of several burthens; one of them will carry twelve or fourteen tons. Timber prepared for building; arms of all sorts for ten men, and burnt by mischance in a house, as much as would have furnished twelve more. John Tailor, 1,500 acres; came over in the summer of 1610, took possession, and remained most part of the following winter; went into England about Shrovetide last, leaving his deputy with some seven or eight tenants; came back about May last with provisions, but went back again; a timber house, with a chimney finished, where he means to erect his dwelling-house. William Snow, 1,500 acres; never came, nor any for him; passed over his proportion to William Lusher, son of Sir Nicholas Lusher; nothing done. Since our return from the North [to Dublin] William Lusher, who bought William Snowe's proportion, came over with his father, took out warrants of possession, and is gone down to his land."

Carew has no report of Sir Nicholas Lusher or Sir Stephen Butler, as these undertakers had probably purchased their lands from other patentees after Carew's inspection. They were noticed, however, with the others, by Pynnar in 1618-1620. Tailor, or Taylor, above-mentioned, had the honour of receiving a communication from the Deputy himself, respecting the site on which he was specially required to erect his residence as a planter. This letter from Chichester is dated Oct. 5, 1611, and is as follows:—"I require you to erect your principal habitation for the present, whether castle or stone house, as you are specially bound, on no other place but at Ballyhaies—parcel of land assigned to you as an undertaker within the County of Cavan—which we understand to be a place of principal advantage for strength and defence of yourself, and other undertakers upon all your precinct. For the more special site we will you to be further advised by Captain Hugh Culme, constable of the King's Castle of Cloughouter, and high sheriff of that county." Taylor had probably insisted on building at some more convenient but less strategic point.

II.

The original plantation landlords thus placed in Loughtee are generally worthy of some further notice. 1. Richard Waldron (afterwards knighted), who purchased his lands in this barony from Sir John Davys, was son of a John Waldron, one of three notorious discoverers who became rich by the plunder of native landowners during the time of Queen Elizabeth's ruthless dealings with Ireland and the Irish. The other two worthies with John Waldron were George Sexten, afterwards Escheator-General in Ulster, and Robert Dixon, one of his assistants. These harpies were in the habit of picking up their prey over a wide field comprehending the Counties of Waterford, Wexford, Meath, Dublin, Kildare, Louth, and Galway, and no fewer than twenty-two native gentlemen were awfully plucked—plucked almost to death by the depredations of this trio of "discoverers," who were able to find fatal flaws in their title-deeds. Richard, the son of John Waldron, must have been thus in a good position to undertake lands and to become a knight. He died in 1623, and his lands were soon afterwards scattered amongst many owners. 2. John Fishe, Esq., came from Bedford, and represented himself as worth £300 a year. He was an energetic planter, and was created a knight as a reward for his liberal expenditure in helping forward the plantation cause on his own immediate property. This honour induced him probably to aspire after another, and by a method, too, which also was supposed to help onward the grand movement—for he soon afterwards got himself dubbed a baronet for the payment of more than £1,000, the proceeds in such cases being ostensibly employed in raising and supporting a standing army in Ulster to protect the settlers from their Irish enemies, whereas, in reality, the money thus supplied found its way in due course, and without unnecessary delay, into the King's private purse. Sir John

Fishe died in March, 1623, and was succeeded by his son, Sir Edward Fishe, who was a popular landlord, and who, in imitation of his father, accepted or admitted many of the Irish as tenants. 3. Sir Stephen Butler came to Cavan from Bedfordshire, and stated that he there owned an estate of some value. His energetic operations at the head of Upper Lough Erne soon secured for him the honour of knighthood. He and all his ancestors were English, although he bore a surname which has long since become almost exceptionally Irish. He was not in any way or degree related to the numerous tribe or clan which has produced so many distinguished Earls and Dukes of Ormonde. Sir Stephen Butler was founder of the family represented by the Earls of Lanesborough, his lady being Mary, a daughter of Gervase Brindsley, of Brindsley, in Nottinghamshire. He died in 1631, leaving a son, James Butler, then ten years of age, in care of three trustees—namely, Sir Robert Dillon, Sir Charles Coote, and Lady Mary Butler, his wife. His son James died in 1640, and a younger son Stephen, then eleven years old, succeeded as next heir. Lady Butler was living in 1638. 4. Sir Nicholas Lusher came from a place called Shooland, in Surrey, but he forfeited his lands in Cavan by neglecting or declining to take the oath of supremacy which all planters were required to take, and also for letting his lands to persons who also neglected or refused to do so. 5. Sir Hugh Worrall came from Enfield, in the County of Middlesex, but there has been already a brief notice of him in connection with his lands in the barony of Clonkelly, County of Fermanagh. 6. John Tailor, or Taylor, came from Cambridgeshire, and was the very first of the planters who was put into possession of lands in Ulster. The Commission for the removal of the natives had commenced its dreadful work first in the County of Cavan, and was opposed by wretched multitudes headed by their brehons or lawyers, who wanted to discuss several burning questions with Chichester, even at the eleventh hour. But Davys explains, or rather affirms, in a letter to Salisbury of Sept. 24, 1610, how nicely Chichester set aside the poor people's despairing efforts to retain their homes :—"Howbeit, my Lord Deputy so mixed threats with entreaty, *precibusque minas regaliter addit*, as that they promised to give way to the undertakers, if the sheriff, by warrant from his Lordship and the Commissioners, put them in possession. Whereupon, his Lordship and the Commissioners signed a warrant to the Sheriff to give possession to one Taylor, an English undertaker, who was then arrived and present in the camp, which warrant was executed without resistance, and thereupon distribution being made to the better sort of natives, of several portions of land in the baronies assigned to them, they not unwillingly accepted of several tickets containing the quantities of land allotted to every particular person. The eyes of all the inhabitants of Ulster were turned upon this County of Cavan, and, therefore, when they saw the difficulty of the business overcome here, their minds were the better prepared to submit themselves to the course prescribed by his Majesty for the plantation." So from one county to another these Commissioners, by order of James I., went on with their work of sowing the dragon's teeth throughout Ulster, which have often bitten so fiercely since, and are not likely to decay or become harmless for some considerable time yet.

From Loughtee the Commissioners of Survey, followed by the Commissioners appointed to mark off the land in proportions, passed into the adjoining barony of Tullyhunco, then Tullochonco. This barony contains the whole parishes of Kildallon, Killeshandra, and Scrabby. Its town and villages are Killeshandra, Arvagh, and Scrabby. By far the greater part of the water area of the barony is comprised in parts of the two loughs, Gawna and

Oughter. Exclusive, however, of this water area, the barony contains 39,000 acres, in which the Commissioners could only find 6,000 acres arable; this was distributed amongst five Scottish planters, with the exception of a very small parcel of Church lands, whilst all the vast remainder was thrown in gratuitously with the five arable proportions. The names of the five planters in Tullyhunco were Sir Alex. Hamilton, knight, of Endervicke, in Scotland; Sir Claude Hamilton, knight, son of the above-named Alexander; Alexander Achmootie, gent.; John Achmootie, gent.; and John Browne, of Gorgiemill, gent. Of the two Hamiltons, father and son, Carew made the following report in 1611:—"Sir Alexander Hamilton, knight, 2,000 acres, in the County of Cavan; has not appeared; his son Claude took possession, and brought two tenants, three servants, and six artificers; is in hand with building a mill; trees felled; hath a minister, but not yet allowed by the Bishop; has raised stones, and hath competent arms in readiness. Besides, there are arrived upon that proportion since our return [to Dublin] from the North, as we are informed, twelve tenants and artificers, who intend to reside there, and build upon the same." The minister brought over by Sir Alexander amongst his other treasures was, no doubt, a Presbyterian, between whom and the Bishop there may have been some sort of compromise before the Scotchman could be permitted "to wag his head" in any pulpit throughout the diocese. These compromises, then occasionally occurring in Ulster, led soon afterwards to frightful wailings and gnashings of teeth between the two parties. Of the two brothers Achmootie, who were servants in the Royal household, Carew reports as fellows:—"John and Alexander Auchmothy, 1,000 acres apiece; have not appeared; James Craige is their deputy for five years, who has brought over four artificers of divers sorts, with their wives and families, and two servants; stone raised for building a mill; trees felled; a walled house with a smith's forge-built; four horses and mares upon the ground; with competent arms." Carew's report of John Browne was "that in 1611 he had sent an agent, who took possession, set the lands to the Irish, returned to Scotland, and had performed nothing."

We meet with Hamiltons here among the planters, as so often elsewhere throughout this province, but how the Hamiltons of Endervicke were related to the Abercorns we cannot say; the former, however, probably belonged to an older family than that settled at Baronscourt. 1. Sir Alex. Hamilton obtained grants in Tullyhunco of the two proportions named Clonkine and Carrotubber, both of which lay between Lough Gawna and the head of Lough-outer. His second son, Sir Claude Hamilton, got one proportion also, but he died before his father, leaving one son, afterwards well known as Sir Francis Hamilton, who succeeded his grandfather in the ownership of the two proportions held by him. In 1618-20 Pynnar found Jane Hamilton, the widow of Sir Claude, in possession of this property, which she held in trust for her son. Sir Claude, the son of Sir Alexander, had sold his proportion of Clonyn in 1611 to John Hamilton, of Corronery, or Hansborough, in the County of Cavan. John Hamilton sold it in turn to William Lawder, of Belhaven, in Scotland; and, on the death of the latter in 1618, it was purchased by Sir Alex. Hamilton, whose heir and grandson, Sir Francis Hamilton, had thus restored to him what had been sold by his father, Sir Claude. Jane Hamilton, the wife of Sir Claude and mother of Sir Francis, remarried with Sir Arthur Forbes, of Granard. 2. The two brothers Achmootie, like almost all the other numerous servants of the King who got shares of the Ulster land spoil, very soon sold their "proportions" of Drumheada and Kilagh to James Craige, their own deputy. Alexander sold his lands on the 14th August, 1610, and John only two days afterwards. Craig, the purchaser, soon distinguished himself as a sort of plantation hero, and, having been also a king's servant, he was forthwith knighted, and encouraged by all means to remain in Ulster. He was soon in a position to purchase other large properties in Cavan, and he, with his wife, Dame Mary, lived in lordly state at their grand residence of Castlecraige. The bordering lands of Sir James Craig and Sir Francis Hamilton became for a time debatable ground on which these knights waged a fierce controversy on the question of mearings. 3. John Browne was another king's servant, although, unlike most others of his class, he appears to have had a Scottish home worthy of being named—if nothing more; he hailed from a place called Gorgiemill. He soon disposed of his "proportion" called Carrodonan, and the Commissioners, or rather Chichester, had a king's letter, dated April 13, 1613, requiring him to "accept a surrender from John Browne, of the manor of Carrodonen, in Cavan County, and to make a grant of the same to Archibald Acheson of Edinburgh, for ever, with the advowson of the church of the Manor." Browne afterwards obtained a lucrative grant from the tolls of the several Ferries in Ulster. Archibald Acheson, the purchaser of Browne's proportion in Tullyhunco, bought up several similar properties, as already mentioned in the County of Armagh. He originally belonged to a place called Gooseford or Guisefoord, in the County of Haddington. He held in succession the several high positions in Scotland of Solicitor-General, Senator of the College of Justice, and Joint Secretary of State. "He kept a large and elegant mansion in the Canongate of Edinburgh, which still remains, presenting over the doorway a crest exhibiting the figure of a cock mounted on a trumpet, with the motto *Vigilantibus*, and the date, 1633. Over two upper windows are the letters

S. A. A. and D. M. H. in large capitals, the initials of Sir Archibald Acheson, and his wife, Dame Margaret Hamilton. Sir Archibald died at Letterkenny, County Donegal, in 1634. He left two sons, viz, Patrick, who succeeded him, and George, third baronet, and owner of the Irish estates." The following notice of Sir Archibald and his family was written after his death by Sir John Scott of Scotstarvet :— "Sir Archibald Acheson, of Glencairney, conjunct-Secretary with the Earl of Stirling, enjoyed the place but few years, and had no land in Scotland, but some four hundred pounds sterling in Ireland of the Earl of Tyrone's lands. His eldest son was of great expectation, having married a rich heiress in England. He died the first year after their marriage, without issue. Of his second wife, Sir William Hamilton's daughter, he had but one son, George; but his mother turned Papist after Sir Archibald's death, and said she had ventured her soul for an Acheson. He died of a pestilential fever; and it is thought that his son George shall get nothing of that estate, it being all destroyed by war in the late [1641] troubles." Sir John Scott was mistaken in supposing that Sir George Acheson would then lose the family property in Ulster. His representatives, now Earls of Gosford, continue to enjoy their broad lands in the counties of Armagh and Cavan at the present day. The Earl now [1876] in possession has offered the Cavan estate in Tullyhunco for sale.

III.

After the barony of Tullyhunco comes that of Clonkee, following the order of the Plantation Commissioners, who wrote its name Clanchy. The surveyors of 1609 only found 6,000 acres of arable land here, although Clonkee contains

64,377 statute acres. This barony comprises the whole parishes of Knockbridge and Shircock, with part of the parishes of Bailieborough, Drumgoon, Ennikeen, and Moybologne. Its towns are Bailieborough and Kingscourt, and its only village is Shircock. Clonkee is situated in the extreme eastern portion of the County of Cavan. Its surface is varied by many lakes, and by a mountain range which runs through the greater portion of the barony, and which shuts out its plantation lands from others that had been appropriated afterwards for a corporate town, a free school, and probably to endow a fort. The 6,000 acres arable were marked off into four proportions, and all the immense remainder of the precinct or barony, being considered "unprofitable," was thrown in gratuitously with these four proportions. Thus the fortunate planters here, as elsewhere generally throughout the six counties, were given ample room and great encouragement to augment and improve their estates. These four proportions fell by lot to the following four Scotchmen, viz.:—Esmy Stuart, Lord Aubigny, William Baillie, Esq.; John Ralestone, gent.; and William Downbarr, or Dunbar, gent. Although the above-named were the original patentees, we shall see that they were, with one exception, soon displaced or superseded by gentlemen bearing the very common but respectable surname of Hamilton. The Hamiltons, in fact, of high and low degree, came literally "as a flood" into Ulster.

Of the four undertakers in Clonkee, Sir George Carew reported, after their first year's occupancy, as follows: — "The Lord Obigny, 3,000 acres in the County of Cavan; appeared not; nor any for him; nothing done; the natives still remaining. William Downbarr, William Baylye, and John Rollestone [or Ralston], 1,000 acres apiece; the like"—*i.e.*, nothing done. 1. Lord Aubigny was second son of Esme Stuart, the first Duke of Lennox, and younger brother of Ludovic, the second Duke. On the death of the latter in February, 1623 24, he succeeded as third Duke, but he only enjoyed the title a few months before his death. He married Katherine, only daughter and heir of Gervase. Lord Clifton, of Leighton Bromewold, by whom he left a numerous family. This lady afterwards married the second Earl of Abercorn, and was granted the right of retaining her rank as Duchess of Lennox. Lord Aubigny got grants of the two proportions of Kinneigh and Cashell, but he did not long retain possession of these lands, as it appears by inquisition that he sold them to Sir James Hamilton, afterwards Lord Clandeboy. 2. It is not known from what place in Scotland William Baillie came, but he proved a good planter on his proportion called Tonneragie, or Tandragee, and he has left his name on a well-known town, indeed the principal town of the barony. There is good evidence that he had made much progress in the interval between the date of Pynnar's inspection, 1618 20, and the holding of an inquisition at Castle-Aubigny, in 1629. It was then found that "Since the graunte of the said premises there is built upon the pole of land called Kilcolhie, *alias* Bailiborrowe, by the said William Baillie and his assigns, one bawne of lyme and stone, and within the said bawne one castell, or fair capital mansion house, built likewise of stone and lyme. The houses are all vaulted belowe, with a staircase and flankers for the defence of the same." The inquisition also informs us of the names of his leaseholders; they were John Steivinson, John Baillie, James Teate, David Barbour, Gilbert Cuthbertson, John Hamilton, William Rae, and Walter Millar. In 1629, he got a re-grant of all his premises, which were created into a manor called Bailiburrowe. 3. John Raleston was another dependent of some sort on the King, but it is not known to what place in Scotland he belonged. He soon sold his proportion.

of Kilologhan to John Hamilton, who had been in possession since 1613. The inquisition at Castle-Aubigny, above quoted, informs us that "John Hamilton had erected upon the lande called Corronerey, *alias* Hansborrowe, a bawne of lyme and stone, twenty foote square, and also another building forty foote long and twenty broade within the walls." It is curious to observe the great discrepancy between the statement in Pynnar's survey and that of the inquisition taken ten years later. Pynnar evidently has told what was intended by Hamilton in the matter of buildings, and we learn from the inquisition that his intentions were very far from being carried out—at least during the time between 1619 and 1629. The inquisition tells us also the names of Hamilton's leaseholders, viz :—Alex. Davyson, Alex. Anderson, John Wyllie, John Musgrave, John and Patrick Finlay, Robert Taillor, John Deanes, and Oliver Udney. Hamilton got a re-grant of all his lands in 1629, which were erected into a manor, to be called the manor of Coronerry, *alias* Hansborough. 4. William Downbarr was another servant or dependent on the King, whose Scottish home is not mentioned, although he appears not to have left it longer than was required to come and take possession of his Ulster estate of 1,000 acres, known as Dromuck. This he soon sold to William Hamilton, a younger brother of Sir James Hamilton, Lord Clandeboy, who had purchased the adjoining lands of Lord Aubigny, as abovementioned. Lord Clandeboy had made a contract with a Dublin grain merchant to supply him from his estate in Clonkee, through the agency of his brother William, but the transaction does not appear to have resulted satisfactorily. In July, 1619, Lord Clandeboy wrote to his brother, and the following extract from his letter plainly enough indicates the dissatisfaction of the writer :—"William,—I have written lately to you by Patrick Shawe, but in good truth not so much as I thinke. I will write no more than that if there be not a greater care had things will fall out that you and I both will be sorry for it; it being strange that of about fourteen hundred pounds sterling, and more, all payable before or at this May day, besides sundry casualties not accounted, I have not hitherto received one penny." This William Hamilton generally resided at Ballymeaghan, now Ballymachan, near Belfast, and was interred in Holywood. He was ancestor of Lord Bangor in the peerage of Ireland.

From Clonkee the Commissioners passed into the adjoining barony of Tullyhaw, then written Tullaghagh, where they found only 9,000 acres arable, although it contains 90,701 statute acres. This barony comprises part of the present parishes of Drumreilly, Kinawley, and Tomregan, with the whole of the parishes of Killinagh and Templeport. The principal villages are Swadlinbar, Ballyconnell, and Bawnboy. Its 9,000 acres arable were marked off into eight proportions, and distributed by lot amongst seven servitors, excepting portions reserved for other plantation purposes, such as small grants to a school and to a fort. The names of the servitors located in this barony were—Sir George and Sir Richard Graham, then written Greame and Grimes; Hugh Culme and Walter Talbott, Esqs.; William Parsons, Esq.; Nicholas Pynnnar, Esq.; and Thomas Johnes, gent. 1. The two Grahams were sons of Sir George Graham, a well-known servitor in Ireland, who came from the Scottish Border, and soon established a claim on the Government by the value and extent of his services. His two sons inherited his unscrupulous dash and courage, distinguishing themselves during the war against the Northern Earls. Towards the close of the reign of James I., Sir Richard Graham and his son William were actively engaged with the connivance and co-operation of Sir William Parsons in the lawless and cruel plunder of two gentleman named O'Byrne, of the County Wicklow. This case, as described by the Protestant historian Carte, presented "such a scene of iniquity and cruelty that it is scarce to be paralleled in any age or country." The story occupies four folio pages in Carte's "Life of the Duke of Ormonde." 2. Hugh Culme and Walter Talbott were both distinguished servitors or soldiers of fortune—one English and the other Irish. Captain Culme, afterwards Sir Hugh Culme, was son of Hugh Culme, of Chamston and Cannonsleigh, in Devonshire. He (Sir Hugh) was Constable of Loughouter Castle, and also held the appointment of Provost-Marshall for the Cavan County and certain surrounding districts. Talbott was greatly recognised and recommended by Chichester; he died in 1625. 3. Nicholas Pynnar, Esq., was known as the author of a survey of the Ulster plantations in the years 1618-1620. 4. William Parsons got a proportion here called Larga, although he had been previously gorged with accumulations of property in land. This proportion was known as the Manor of Pinner and Parsontowne, and was composed of several parcels of concealed lands. On this account Parson was not bound to build on it, so his rents from it were profits without any outlay.

The Commissioners next commenced proceedings in the barony of Clonmahon, where servitors and natives were to be located as in the precinct or barony of Clonkee. Clonmahon contains 54,346 acres, and comprises the whole of the parishes of Ballintemple, Drumlonan, and Ballymachugh, with part of the parishes of Crosserlough, Denn, Kilbride, and Kilmore. The beautiful Lough Sheelin is almost the one attractive feature in this region. The baronial map of 1609 represents the surface as a network of woods and bogs, and the Commissioners could only find about 7,000 acres of arable land therein. This quantity was marked off into six proportions and allotted to four servitors. Their names were Sir Oliver Lambert, Knight;

Joseph Jones, gent. ; John Russon, gent. ; and Anthony Atkinson, gent. 1. Sir Oliver Lambert came to Ireland in 1581 ; he was grandson of Richard Lambert, grocer, merchant adventurer, alderman, and sheriff of London. He is said to have belonged to the Lambertini family, and that his ancestor Ralph de Lambert came to England with William the Conqueror. However this may be, it is certain that Sir Oliver advanced rapidly in the service here—so rapidly, indeed, that in 1601 he was appointed Governor of Connaught. That unhappy province he thoroughly revolutionised, so far as seizing much of its lands and expelling the rightful owners could be described as doing so. The several inquisitions taken after his death revealed the prodigious amount of territory he had clutched, not only in Cavan, but in at least a dozen other counties in Ireland. 2. Joseph Johnes or Jones was one of the numerous and hungry swarm of adventurers bearing this surname who invaded Ireland from Wales early in the seventeenth century. Descendants of Joseph Jones rose into repute and respectability at Headfort, in the adjoining County of Leitrim, and not very distant from the manor of Tocullen, which was allotted to him as a servitor in the barony of Clonmahon. In this Leitrim family the Christian name Theophilus prevailed, which would lead to the conclusion that it was a brand of the same stock from which came the famous, or rather infamous, Bishop Jones, who acted as Cromwell's scoutmaster in Ireland, and who had a younger brother named Theophilus. 3. John Russon—probably a mistake for John Russell—as this servitor's name is written by Pynnar. He got 500 acres, which he sold to Archibald Moore, another servitor, and on which the latter in Pynnar's report is said to have built a bawne of sodds, with an Irish house inside. 4. Anthony Atkinson was probably a brother of Roger Atkinson, also a servitor, who got a "proportion" in Fermanagh. A lieutenant

Anthony Atkinson settled at a place called Kiltobret, King's County, about the year 1602, and, from intermarriages in his family with families in the County of Cavan, we are disposed to believe that he was the undertaker here mentioned in Clonmahon. One of his representatives married a daughter of Robert Saunderson, Cloverhill, County of Cavan; another married a granddaughter of Sir Francis Hamilton, of Killeshandra, same county; and a third married a daughter of Sir Robert Newcomen, who owned an estate in the escheated lands of the adjoining County of Tyrone. Branches of this Atkinson family are seated at Cangort, in King's County, and Ashley Park, in the County of Tipperary.

IV.

From Clonmahon the Commissioners passed into the adjoining barony of Castlerahen—a name now written Castle-Rahan. This precinct also, like the three others in Cavan allotted to servitors and natives, was exceptionally bleak and uninteresting as a general rule, although it contained pleasant corners to be occupied by servitors. On the map of 1609 "Logh Rawre," now Lough Ramor, is represented as having nine islands, some of which appear very small. On one island there were the ruins of a church, and on the southern shore of the lough there were, according to the map, the remains of a castle or fortress. The surface generally appears then to have been rather profusely supplied with marshes, bleak-looking little hills, and bogs. Hardly a tree appears on the whole expanse of about 70,000 acres. The ruins of "Caslan-Rahan" are marked on the map as near the base of the "Slew M'Kaffry Mountains," on the borders of Munster. This barony comprises the whole of the present parishes of Castle Rahan, Lurgan, Mullough, and Munterconnaght, with part of the parishes of Bailieborough, Crosserlogh, Denn, Killinere, and Loughan. It contains the towns of Ballyjamesduff and Virginia; and the villages of Kilnalock and Mullagh.

The surveyors only found 9,000 acres arable in Castle-Rahan, which quantity was marked off into six proportions and distributed amongst five planters of the servitor class. All the vast remainder of over 60,000 acres (except a trifling amount divided amongst some natives) was thrown in gratuitously with the six proportions. The following are the names of the servitors to which these proportions were allotted, viz.:—Sir John Elliot, knight; John Ridgeway, Esq.; Sir William Taaffe, knight; Roger Garth, gent.; and Sir Edmund Fettiplace, knight. Of these servitors Carew reports in 1611:—"Sir William Tathe [Taaffe], knight, 1,000 acres, as servitor at Castle Rame, has taken possession, but nothing done. Sir Edmund Fetiplace has taken possession, nothing else done. Lieut. Garth, 500 acres as servitor, has taken possession, but nothing done. Captain John Ridgeway, 1,000 acres; 120 great oaks have been brought from Fermanagh, thirty miles from him, and more ready framed, being 280 garrons' loads from Bealturberte; has made a watercourse for a mill in a stony and rocky ground, which cost him £25, as he says; has agreed for 500 barrels of lime in Meath, to be brought him upon demand; has removed five Irish houses near his castle, and built two other Irish houses on the great island [in Lough Ramor]; has an English millwright, smith, and farrier, with their wives and families, and necessary tools; and an English and Irish house carpenter, with their wives and families; two or three other families of several trades; and has contracted at Bealturberte for a boat for use on Lough Rawre" [Ramor].

These gentlemen crowded as much as possible around the shores of Lough Ramor, for there lay almost all the good lands in the barony. 1. Sir John Elliot was a distinguished English lawyer, and if, in this dividing of the Ulster land spoil, he appears to have got a small proportion, at least in Castle-Rahan, he had a large share in the work of hunting it out. In a "Briefe" abstract of all the extraordinary payments in the year ending September, 1608, there is the following item :—"Baron Elliot, for his charges and pains sustained in finding sundry indictments against the fugitive Earls, £20." In a list of "allowances made by way of concordatum" during the year ending April 14, 1609, there is the following entry :—"Sir John Elliot, one of the Barons of the Court, by two concordatums, £76." On a list containing the names of "Judges and Law Officers, with their fees," Elliot's fee is £66 13s 4d; his robes, £13 6s 8d. 2. John Ridgeway was a younger brother of Sir Thomas and of George Ridgeway, already mentioned in connection with the barony of Clogher, in Tyrone. He was classed "among those servitors who were not in pay, but willing to undertake," and it might have been truly added that such were not merely "willing" but quite anxious to become undertakers. Although he had made good progress as a planter during the first year of his occupancy, he sold his lands in Castle-Rahan to Captain Hugh Culme, of whom we have already heard as an undertaker in a neighbouring barony. Sir Hugh Culme was related to Chichester by his mother, who was a daughter of Richard Fortescue, of Fileigh, in Devonshire. Culme was Constable of Loughouter Castle, and afterwards occupied it as a private residence. He died in 1630, and by his wife, who remarried with Colonel Jones, he left a large family of sons and daughters, one of his daughters married John Edgeworth, of Cranelagh, in Longford; and another daughter married George Bradshaw, of Bradshaw, in Derbyshire. Sir Hugh Culme's proportion, called Logh-Rammar, was erected into a manor, known as the Manor of Chichester, and, when obtaining these lands, he engaged to build a town called Virginia, for which he was allowed 250 acres. "Upon this," says Pynnar, "he hath built 8 timber houses, and put in them 8 English tenants; of which town there is a minister which keepeth school, and is a very good preacher." It does not appear why Sir Hugh Culme selected the name Virginia for his little town, but it has remained in use ever since. Virginia stands on the north-eastern shore of Lough Ramor, and belongs to the Headfort estate, the lords of which, in their generations, had the place duly cared for, and made attractive. The inn at Virginia was once spoken of as being the best on the whole line of road from Enniskillen to Dublin. The "good preacher," who settled there for a time, was Benjamin Culme, a brother of Sir Hugh. In 1615 this clergyman was appointed prebend of St. Malahide; in 1616, rector of Rathmore; and in 1619, Dean of St. Patrick's, Dublin. 3. 4. 5. Sir William Taaffe, Roger Garth, and Sir Edmund Fettiplace severally sold out their proportions to Sir Thomas Ashe.

Tullaghgarvey, the only remaining barony of County Cavan to be mentioned, was allotted, like the three preceding ones, to servitors and natives, for certain special reasons. It contained several good positions for defence, should tumults have happened to arise, and these positions, with their adjoining lands, the best in the barony, were given to the servitors. The remaining lands of Tullaghgarvey were the most barren, perhaps, in the whole County of Cavan, and were, therefore, considered quite good enough for such natives throughout the county as had got small patches of freehold. The barony in general retains, even at the present day, its former bleak aspect and comparatively barren soil. But the homes of the servitors in its eastern corner around Cootehill, and in its western corner around Castle Saunderson, and in the pleasant valley of the Annalee, were attractive enough as contrasted with the surrounding and intervening sterility. The barony contains about 60,000 acres, exclusive of the water surface, and comprises part of the parishes of Annagh, Drumgoon, and Laragh, with the whole of the parishes of Drung and Kildrumsherdon.

The Commissioners of Survey could only find 7,500 arable acres in Tullaghgarvey, which quantity was marked off into seven proportions, and distributed, with slight exceptions, amongst five servitors, whose names were Sir Thomas Ashe, Knight; John Ashe, gent.; Archibald Moore, and Brent, gents.; Richard Tyrrell, Esq.; and Mulmorie, or Myles, O'Reilly, who obtained a portion of his own lands, but only on plantation conditions. 1. Sir Thomas and John Ashe were brothers, and the sons of Thomas Ashe by his wife Mary, a daughter of Nicholas Bailey, of St. John's Abbey, County of Meath. Thomas, the elder son, was knighted by Sir George Carew in 1603, and he was also substantially rewarded for his services in the war against the Northern Earls. With other good things Sir Thomas Ashe obtained the wardship of an Irish gentleman's heir named O'Carroll, but he found that business becoming troublesome, and therefore disposed of it soon, and on as good terms for himself as possible. The following reference to this transaction by Chichester in January 1609-10 is instructive as explanatory of the means employed through the agency of "discoverers" to ruin native landowners:—"Patrick Crosbye [a discoverer] tells me that the Lord Treasurer had some speech with him about Ely O Carroll, *alias* O'Carroll's country, which I have made shire ground, and laid to the King's County. It is a pretty piece of land, and Crosbye says he can bring it into the King's hands by overthrowing [discovering flaws in] the patent thereof made to Sir William O'Carroll. The pretending heir is an infant, whose wardship was given to Sir Thomas Ashe before my time. There has ever been strife and contention between the house of Ormonde and the lords of that country [Ely O'Carroll], touching the bounds and meares, and much blood spilt on either side, and now I am told that Sir Thomas Ashe has sold over the ward [O'Carroll's son and heir] to the Viscount Butler, notwithstanding my advice to him not to deal therewith, and to Sir Thomas Ashe not to sell it to him; for I doubted the sequel as I still do, but still I wish well to the Viscount, who is an honest gentleman. But I would not have his power and liberty increased on that side of the country bordering upon Tipperary; and, therefore, if Crosbye can bring the country to the Crown he deserves a good recompense. For this service he deserves one-half of the country [Ely O'Carroll] in fee farm, at £50 English." This was Chichester's practical way of settling matters against the natives, and by this policy Crosby and such villains as he soon became rich and high in rank, whilst Sir William O'Carroll and such native landlords as he very quickly sunk into beggary and ruin. 2. Archibald and Brent Moore came from Bennenden, in the County of Kent, as had also come the Moores of Drogheda. John, the representative of the family at the close of the sixteenth century, married Margaret, the daughter and heir of John Brent, by whom he had six sons. The second son, Sir Edward Moore, of Mellifont, was ancestor of the Earls of Drogheda; the fourth son, Sir Thomas Moore, of Croghan, was ancestor of the Earls of Charleville; and the sixth son, Colonel Brent Moore, was an undertaker of lands in the plantation of Longford. He probably dwelt on his Longford estate, as his name does not afterwards appear in any Ulster inquisition yet printed. Of these two brothers who got shares in the plantation spoils, Archibald was probably the elder, for he had become well known as a servitor;

whilst Brent, although a soldier, does not appear to have been included in any of the several classes into which Ulster servitors were divided. 3. Mulmorie O'Reilly, the youthful representative of the whole clan or sept of O'Reilly, did not live long after getting his plantation grant from the Government. His mother, who was a niece of the Earl of Ormonde, retired with her son, then only a boy, to their proportion of Ballincairge, the name also of an old castle built there many centuries previously by one of his ancestors. Although Pynnar speaks of him as if he had been alive in 1618, it was found by an inquisition at Belturbet in 1622 that he had died in February, 1617. His trustees, appointed in 1612, were Walter Talbott, of Ballaconelly, in the County of Cavan; Thomas Brady, of Drogheda, merchant; and Arthur M'Gra, of Ballincairge. Other native gentlemen who got somewhat liberal grants are reported by Sir George Carew as follows:—"Hugh M'Shane O'Reilly removed to his portion and is building a mill. Melmore M'Philip O'Reilly removed and is building a house. Connor Shane Roe M'Brady removed to his proportion. Melmore M'Hugh Conelagh O'Reilly is dwelling on the land he had before, and given him on the last division. M'Kyernan removed to his proportion, and is about building a house. Brian M'Owen removed to his proportion. Philip M'Tirlagh Brady is about to remove. Magauran had his own land given to him on this division. Rest of the natives that had lands assigned to them in Cavan not yet removed. In the case of these influential natives, the great and most important point with the Government was their voluntarily, and without force, removing. The humbler classes, it was hoped, would thus the sooner disappear before the coming settlers. Only fifty-five natives in the County of Cavan obtained small grants from the Crown in the three several baronies already mentioned. Several of these, as in the counties preceding, represented noble

Irish families, whilst the remaining grantees belonged to the native gentry class. Their surnames most common amongst this lot of native grantees were O'Reilly, Magauran, O'Brady, and Mackernan.

NOTE.—The adjoining County of Monaghan was one of the three not included in the plantation, because, as in the cases of Antrim and Down, it had been settled after a fashion some years before. The story of its settlement, however, may be soon told, for the means employed in perpetrating the same were peculiarly sharp and simple. On the dismissal and attainder of Sir John Perrot, Chichester's father-in-law, Dublin Castle was occupied for the third time, or turn, by Sir William Fitzwilliam, who was, perhaps, the basest of the many base Lord Deputies inflicted on Ireland, for he never scrupled any meanness or atrocity which assisted in filling his own pockets. Fitzwilliam was originally sent to this country to lend a hand in the management of the Crown property, which was then enormous, and whilst thus employed he had become a thorough expert in the art or science of public plunder. At all events, his "intimate knowledge of Ireland" induced Elizabeth to appoint him to the office of Lord Deputy, in the year 1559; and, unfortunately for hapless Ireland, Fitzwilliam took to liking her so devotedly, that he intrigued and cajoled to any amount, until he got himself appointed a second, and even a third time. In this instance we have a specially good illustration of the Queen's well recognised policy of sending her vultures to Ireland whilst she let fly her eagles at Spain. Amongst Fitzwilliam's congenial exploits during his long and fatal connection with this country was his settlement of Monaghan, by the murder of its chief, and the distribution of the clansmen's lands principally to his own flagitious agents and assistants. Of these men (among whom Sir Henry Bagnall figured prominently) we have the following account from Captain Thomas Lee, an English gentleman and a faithful servitor in Ireland for the space of twenty years: —"His [Fitzwilliam's] greedy desire at that time, in respect of his own gain, made him esteem the baser sort of servitors, whom he made captains and officers in the Irish countries, who, with their great troops of base rascals, behaved themselves so disorderly as made the whole country to rise in an uproar and drive them out, which example, given by those bad and lewd fellows, to the ill disposed Irishry, hath embolden them ever since to stand in no fear or subjection."

On the death of Ross MacMahon, the territorial Lord of Monaghan, there appeared likely to arise feuds among the clansmen as to his successor; but, irrespective of the clansmen's opinions or wishes on the subject, Fitzwilliam appointed Hugh Roe, a younger brother of the deceased, as The MacMahon. The successful candidate was able to offer larger bribes to the Lord Deputy than any of the others, and actually handed over to Fitzwilliam eight hundred head of cattle—five hundred for himself, and one hundred and fifty each for his wife and son. But MacMahon's lands were wanted as well as his cattle—so a ready pretext for his destruction soon turned up. Hugh Roe, on being regularly recognised as The MacMahon, proceeded to enforce the payment of certain rents, according to the forms prescribed by the Celtic law in such cases—for as yet the English law had not been regularly introduced, and was not therefore available. Yet, in appealing to the old Irish law, MacMahon's act was interpreted as a contravention of the prerogative of the Crown—as, in fact, a case of high treason. He was forthwith summoned to Dublin, in an apparently friendly spirit, and on going there was seized and soon afterwards executed without having had any time or means to provide for his defence. This tragedy was rendered the more impressive and appalling by the fact that Fitzwilliam sent back his victim to Monaghan alive, and had him hanged at the entrance to his [MacMahon's] own castle. The latter had attempted too freely and publicly to make capital out of his bribes to the whole Fitzwilliam party in Dublin Castle, thus bringing upon himself the swifter destruction. His foul murder, and the subsequent distribution of most of his estates amongst Fitzwilliam's emissaries, are detailed in the following terms in the well-known "Statement of Grievances," laid before Elizabeth by two most respectable members of the MacMahon family :—"First, Hugh Roe, named The MacMahon by Sir William Fitzwilliam, and so confirmed and allowed to succeed, on coming in to the State [going to Dublin] on the word of a nobleman, and on the word of Henry Moore, of Mellifont, was afterwards most unjustly and most treacherously executed at his own house of Monaghan. The allowance of succession was granted to him, the said Hugh Roe, purposely to draw an interest unto him and his heirs, contrary to the custom of the country, and then by his execution to draw the country into her Majesty's hands, as the sequel showeth. After his execution a garrison was placed in Monaghan, the name [title] of The MacMahon extinguished, and the county divided by Fitzwilliam between Sir Henry Bagnall, Baron Elliott, Mr. Solicitor Wilbraham, Captain Henshaw, Captain Wallis, the Parson O'Connelan, Hugh Strowbridge, Thomas Ashe, Charles Fleming, and divers other strangers ; and so the native country people for the most part disinherited, and some of those that had portions allotted to them were afterwards murdered—namely, Patrick MacMahon coming on safe conduct to the Parson O'Connelan, then justice of peace and chief man in authority, was intercepted by an ambush laid by the said Parson and Captain Wallis, and there slain." The divers strangers who got large portions of the lands in Monaghan, but who are not named in the foregoing document, were Roger Garlon, of Strabannan, in the County of Louth; Thomas Clinton, of Dowdstown, in the County of Louth; William Garvey, son to the Lord Primate; and Gerald Dillon, of Ardbraccan.

Whilst the whole country was aflame, and taking counsel to avenge this and other aggressions equally foul and oppressive, Fitzwilliam returned to England in triumph and burdened with enormous spoils. Although he was nominally arraigned for his crimes, the Lords of the Council in London took good care that he should be held not only scatheless, but that he should receive distinguished honours for having drawn Monaghan "into her Majesty's hands." Fitzwilliam's conduct was thus thoroughly condoned, and his "monstrous and apparent untruths"—as Captain Lee termed his statements before the Council in London—were ll accepted as great and most gratifying political intelligence from Ireland. And the grand culprit himself knew well how to justify his conduct in the murder of MacMahon. He was silent about the bribes he had received from Hugh Roe, and defended himself solely on the grounds of his loyal devotedness to the best interests of the Crown! The following is his explanation to the old tyrant Burghley, President of the Council, in March, 1589:—"As I never benefited myself by MacMahon's admission [to the headship of his clan], so do I mean to convert his fall wholly to the profit of her Majesty and the good of the State, not regarding mine own private. I speak it as in the presence of God, by whom I hope to be saved." No English chronicler, as far as we know, not even Camden, has ventured to defend this business, which was indeed the principal cause of the seven years' frightful war against the Northern Lords; and which remains, and will ever remain, one of the many indelible stains on the English rule in Ireland. And, as a ghastly memento in Monaghan of Fitzwilliam's horrible crime, it may be mentioned, in conclusion, that the walls of MacMahon's castle still remain and the oak tree on which he was hanged is yet alive. It stands on one side of the ancient avenue, and only a few perches from the ruins of the castle.